Photoshop CS6:
Basic
Student Manual

ACE Edition

Photoshop CS6: Basic

Chief Executive Officer, Axzo Press:	Ken Wasnock
Series Designer and COO:	Adam A. Wilcox
Vice President, Operations:	Josh Pincus
Director of Publishing Systems Development:	Dan Quackenbush
Writer:	Chris Hale
Keytester:	Lori Minnehan

Trademarks

ILT Series is a trademark of Axzo Press.

Some of the product names and company names used in this book have been used for identification purposes only and may be trademarks or registered trademarks of their respective manufacturers and sellers.

Disclaimer

We reserve the right to revise this publication and make changes from time to time in its content without notice.

ISBN 10: 1-4260-3550-0
ISBN 13: 978-1-4260-3550-0

Printed in the United States of America

1 2 3 4 5 GL 06 05 04 03

Contents

Introduction

After reading this introduction, you will know how to:

A Use ILT Series manuals in general.

B Use prerequisites, a target student description, course objectives, and a skills inventory to properly set your expectations for the course.

C Re-key this course after class.

Topic A: About the manual

ILT Series philosophy

Our manuals facilitate your learning by providing structured interaction with the software itself. While we provide text to explain difficult concepts, the hands-on activities are the focus of our courses. By paying close attention as your instructor leads you through these activities, you will learn the skills and concepts effectively.

We believe strongly in the instructor-led class. During class, focus on your instructor. Our manuals are designed and written to facilitate your interaction with your instructor, and not to call attention to manuals themselves.

We believe in the basic approach of setting expectations, delivering instruction, and providing summary and review afterwards. For this reason, lessons begin with objectives and end with summaries. We also provide overall course objectives and a course summary to provide both an introduction to and closure on the entire course.

Manual components

The manuals contain these major components:

- Table of contents
- Introduction
- Units
- Appendix
- Course summary
- Glossary
- Index

Each element is described below.

Table of contents

The table of contents acts as a learning roadmap.

Introduction

The introduction contains information about our training philosophy and our manual components, features, and conventions. It contains target student, prerequisite, objective, and setup information for the specific course.

Units

Units are the largest structural component of the course content. A unit begins with a title page that lists objectives for each major subdivision, or topic, within the unit. Within each topic, conceptual and explanatory information alternates with hands-on activities. Units conclude with a summary comprising one paragraph for each topic, and an independent practice activity that gives you an opportunity to practice the skills you've learned.

The conceptual information takes the form of text paragraphs, exhibits, lists, and tables. The activities are structured in two columns, one telling you what to do, the other providing explanations, descriptions, and graphics.

Appendix

The appendix for this course lists the Adobe Certified Expert (ACE) exam objectives for Photoshop CS6, along with references to corresponding coverage in ILT Series courseware.

Course summary

This section provides a text summary of the entire course. It is useful for providing closure at the end of the course. The course summary also indicates the next course in this series, if there is one, and lists additional resources you might find useful as you continue to learn about the software.

Glossary

The glossary provides definitions for all of the key terms used in this course.

Index

The index at the end of this manual makes it easy for you to find information about a particular software component, feature, or concept.

Manual conventions

We've tried to keep the number of elements and the types of formatting to a minimum in the manuals. This aids in clarity and makes the manuals more classically elegant looking. But there are some conventions and icons you should know about.

Item	Description
Italic text	In conceptual text, indicates a new term or feature.
Bold text	In unit summaries, indicates a key term or concept. In an independent practice activity, indicates an explicit item that you select, choose, or type.
`Code font`	Indicates code or syntax.
`Longer strings of ▶ code will look ▶ like this.`	In the hands-on activities, any code that's too long to fit on a single line is divided into segments by one or more continuation characters (▶). This code should be entered as a continuous string of text.
Select **bold item**	In the left column of hands-on activities, bold sans-serif text indicates an explicit item that you select, choose, or type.
Keycaps like (↵ ENTER)	Indicate a key on the keyboard you must press.

Hands-on activities

The hands-on activities are the most important parts of our manuals. They are divided into two primary columns. The "Here's how" column gives short instructions to you about what to do. The "Here's why" column provides explanations, graphics, and clarifications. Here's a sample:

Do it!

A-1:   Creating a commission formula

Here's how	Here's why
1 Open Sales	This is an oversimplified sales compensation worksheet. It shows sales totals, commissions, and incentives for five sales reps.
2 Observe the contents of cell F4	F4 ▾ = =E4*C_Rate The commission rate formulas use the name "C_Rate" instead of a value for the commission rate.

For these activities, we have provided a collection of data files designed to help you learn each skill in a real-world business context. As you work through the activities, you will modify and update these files. Of course, you might make a mistake and therefore want to re-key the activity starting from scratch. To make it easy to start over, you will rename each data file at the end of the first activity in which the file is modified. Our convention for renaming files is to add the word "My" to the beginning of the file name. In the above activity, for example, a file called "Sales" is being used for the first time. At the end of this activity, you would save the file as "My sales," thus leaving the "Sales" file unchanged. If you make a mistake, you can start over using the original "Sales" file.

In some activities, however, it might not be practical to rename the data file. If you want to retry one of these activities, ask your instructor for a fresh copy of the original data file.

Topic B: Setting your expectations

Properly setting your expectations is essential to your success. This topic will help you do that by providing:

- Prerequisites for this course
- A description of the target student
- A list of the objectives for the course
- A skills assessment for the course

Course prerequisites

Before taking this course, you should be familiar with personal computers and the use of a keyboard and a mouse. Furthermore, this course assumes that you've completed the following courses or have equivalent experience:

- *Windows 7: Basic*

Target student

The target student for this course is someone who is familiar with computers and who wants to use Adobe Photoshop to create and modify digital images, such as digital-camera images or scanned photographs or artwork. After completing this course, you will be able to use Photoshop CS6 to select part of an image, use layers, apply image adjustments, retouch and repair photographs, and use Adobe Bridge to view and organize files.

Adobe ACE certification

This course is designed to help you pass the Adobe Certified Expert (ACE) exam for Photoshop CS6. For complete certification training, you should complete this course and all of the following:

- *Photoshop CS6: Advanced, ACE Edition*
- *Photoshop CS6: Production, ACE Edition*

Course objectives

These overall course objectives will give you an idea about what to expect from the course. It is also possible that they will help you see that this course is not the right one for you. If you think you either lack the prerequisite knowledge or already know most of the subject matter to be covered, you should let your instructor know that you think you are misplaced in the class.

After completing this course, you will know how to:

- Understand different file types used in Photoshop and save files, customize the Photoshop environment, magnify and scroll images, set up rulers and guides, specify tool options, and create and export tool presets.

- Use several selection tools to select image areas; and modify and manipulate selections.

- Create, arrange, and transform layers; create type layers; and use opacity and layer styles to apply effects to layer contents.

- Add adjustment layers, apply automatic adjustments, locate image shadows and highlights, set target points in a Levels adjustment layer, and use a Curves adjustment layer to adjust image contrast.

- Repair image defects, retouch images, erase complex background areas and use Content-Aware Fill, paint in an image, and apply filters to a layer or selection.

- Determine an image's resolution and dimensions, resize images with and without resampling, and use the Crop tool and the Canvas Size command to change an image's canvas size.

- Use Adobe Bridge to import files, navigate your computer's folder structure, review files, view and modify file metadata, create collections, and output files by creating PDFs and Web galleries.

Skills inventory

Use the following form to gauge your skill level entering the class. For each skill listed, rate your familiarity from 1 to 5, with five being the most familiar. *This is not a test.* Rather, it is intended to provide you with an idea of where you're starting from at the beginning of class. If you're wholly unfamiliar with all the skills, you might not be ready for the class. If you think you already understand all of the skills, you might need to move on to the next course in the series. In either case, you should let your instructor know as soon as possible.

Skill	1	2	3	4	5
Saving a file in Photoshop format					
Saving an image for Web use					
Organizing Photoshop panels					
Magnifying and scrolling images					
Setting up guides, rulers, and grids					
Selecting image areas by using various tools and commands					
Adding to and subtracting from a selection					
Modifying a selection					
Creating layers and moving layers between images					
Arranging and transforming layers					
Creating type layers and formatting text					
Adjusting layer opacity by using the Layers panel					
Applying layer styles					
Creating adjustment layers by using the Adjustments panel					
Locating image shadows and highlights					
Setting target points					
Using a Levels adjustment layer					
Using a Curves adjustment layer					
Fixing red-eye					
Using the Clone Stamp tool and the Clone Source panel					
Using the Spot Healing Brush and Patch tools					

Skill	1	2	3	4	5
Using the Background Eraser tool					
Filling selections by using Content-Aware Fill					
Using the Content-Aware Move tool					
Painting with the History brush					
Specifying the foreground and background colors					
Sampling colors with the Eyedropper tool					
Painting in an image by using the Brush tool					
Applying filters					
Determining an image's dimensions and resolution					
Resizing and resampling images by using the Image Size command					
Adjusting canvas size by using the Crop tool and the Canvas Size command					
Importing images in Bridge					
Viewing and modifying metadata					
Creating collections					
Creating a contact sheet and a Web gallery					

Topic C: Re-keying the course

If you have the proper hardware and software, you can re-key this course after class. This section explains what you'll need in order to do so, and how to do it.

Hardware requirements

Your personal computer should have:

- A keyboard and a mouse
- Intel Pentium 4 or AMD Athlon 64 Processor (or faster)
- 1GB RAM (or higher)
- 1 GB of available hard drive space after the operating system is installed
- A monitor with at least 1280×960 resolution
- A graphics display card chip (GPU) that supports OpenGL (**Note:** Activities will still work without OpenGL support, but some features won't be enabled.)

Software requirements

You will also need the following software:

- Microsoft Windows 7 (You can also use Windows XP, but the screenshots in this course were taken in Windows 7, so your screens might look somewhat different.)
- Adobe Photoshop CS6
- A display driver that supports OpenGL 2.0 and Shader Model 3.0 (**Note:** Activities will still work without OpenGL support, but some features won't be enabled.)

Network requirements

The following network components and connectivity are also required for re-keying this course:

- Internet access, for the following purposes:
  - Downloading the latest critical updates and service packs
  - Downloading the Student Data files (if necessary)

Setup instructions to re-key the course

Before you re-key the course, you will need to perform the following steps.

1   Use Windows Update to install all available critical updates and service packs.

2   With flat-panel displays, we recommend using the panel's native resolution for best results. Color depth/quality should be set to High (24 bit) or higher.

   Please note that your display settings or resolution may differ from the author's, so your screens might not exactly match the screenshots in this manual.

3   If necessary, reset any Photoshop defaults that you have changed. To do so, when starting Photoshop, hold down Shift+Ctrl+Alt until the dialog box appears, asking if you want to delete the settings file; click Yes. (If you do not wish to reset the defaults, you can still re-key the course, but some activities might not work exactly as documented.)

4   Configure Photoshop CS6 as follows:

   a   Start Photoshop.

   b   Choose Edit, Preferences, File Handling.

   c   Under File Compatibility, set Maximize PSD and PSB Compatibility to Always. Click OK.

   d   Close Photoshop.

5   If you have the data disc that came with this manual, locate the Student Data folder on it and copy it to your Windows desktop.

   If you don't have the data disc, you can download the Student Data files for the course:

   a   Connect to http://downloads.logicaloperations.com.

   b   Enter the course title or search by part to locate this course

   c   Click the course title to display a list of available downloads.
       Note: Data Files are located under the Instructor Edition of the course.

   d   Click the link(s) for downloading the Student Data files.

   e   Create a folder named Student Data on the desktop of your computer.

   f   Double-click the downloaded zip file(s) and drag the contents into the Student Data folder.

U n i t 1

Getting started

Complete this unit, and you'll know how to:

A Understand different file types used in Photoshop and save files.

B Customize the Photoshop environment to appear the way you want; magnify and scroll images; and set up rulers, guides, and grids.

C Specify tool options and create and export tool presets.

Topic A: File types

This topic covers the following ACE exam objectives for Photoshop CS6.

#	Objective
10.1	**Differentiating between file types**
10.1.1	Understanding the differences between TIF, JPG, PNG, GIF, PSD, PSB, and other file types
10.1.2	Understanding which file type to choose for a given scenario

Photoshop file formats

Explanation

Photoshop supports a number of file formats, and it's important to use the correct file type for the job. Although the number of formats can be overwhelming, fortunately you'll typically use only a handful, or maybe even two or three.

PSD format

If you want to be sure to preserve all the features you'll use when working with images in Photoshop, then the best file format is the one native to Photoshop: PSD. However, some applications into which you'll be importing finished images might not support PSD files; in addition, PSD files that contain layers and other elements can have very large file sizes, making them inappropriate for Web use, for example.

Therefore, it might be a good idea to keep the original PSD files somewhere safe, in case you need to go back and make further adjustments. But for uses outside of Photoshop, other formats might be more appropriate. Some of the most commonly used file types are JPEG, GIF, PNG, and TIFF.

JPEG images

A JPEG (or .jpg) image can display millions of colors, and the JPEG format compresses image data to generate a file that's much smaller than the original Photoshop file. The JPEG compression is *lossy*, which means that it discards image data to compress the image. This process can introduce image distortions. However, when you specify the JPEG format, you can specify a quality setting. A higher-quality setting generates an image with less distortion but a larger file size. A lower-quality setting generates an image with more distortion but a smaller file size.

JPEG images typically are used in Web applications, but they can also be suitable for print. Unlike some other formats, JPEG doesn't support transparency.

GIF images

A GIF image can display a maximum of 256 colors, so it's typically not appropriate for continuous-tone images such as photographs. However, the GIF format uses *lossless* compression, which decreases file size without introducing any distortion.

GIF images are used primarily for Web applications, especially for graphics with few colors and for animations.

PNG images

The PNG image format combines some of the best features of JPEG and GIF. It supports more than 16 million colors, so it's ideal for photos and complex drawings. It can use a variety of lossless compression algorithms, and it supports many levels of transparency, allowing areas of an image to appear transparent or semi-transparent.

PNG images are suitable for Web and for print use, although some Web browsers might not fully support the format's transparency settings.

TIFF images

The TIFF format is compatible with most other applications and is suitable for high-quality printing. TIFF images preserve layers created in Photoshop, which gives you flexibility when using the images in applications such as InDesign that support Photoshop layers. TIFF images typically aren't suitable for Web use, however.

The Save As dialog box

When you open and edit a file, you have a few options for saving it. To save a file, you can choose File, Save to save it in the current format and with the current file name, or you can choose File, Save As to open the Save As dialog box, shown in Exhibit 1-1.

If the original file format doesn't support layers, then (assuming you've added layers) you'll be prompted to save the file in Photoshop format. You can choose to save the file in its original format instead, and, depending on whether the format supports them, you can choose whether to preserve layers.

You can use Photoshop to save an image, with all of its layers, in TIFF format, but because some applications can't properly import TIFF images with layers, it's best to clear Layers in the Save As dialog box. Flattening an image to a single layer also reduces the image's file size. Again, it's also a good idea to save the PSD format as well, in case you need to make further adjustments to the image.

Because some commands, such as those that apply filters, can't be applied to multiple layers, you might want to flatten layers for an image even if you're not saving it in another format. However, you should always keep a copy of the image with all layers so you can return to it for any further modifications.

To flatten all layers, do either of the following:

- From the Layers panel menu, choose Flatten Image.
- Choose Layer, Flatten Image.

Exhibit 1-1: The Save As dialog box, displaying file formats

Do it!

A-1: Saving a file in Photoshop format

The files for this activity are in Student Data folder **Unit 1\Topic A**.

Here's how	Here's why
1 Click [icon]	(The Start button.) To display the Start menu.
Click **All Programs**	To display the All Programs submenu.
Choose **Adobe Photoshop CS6**	To start Adobe Photoshop CS6. A folder containing Photoshop CS6 might be present if the program was installed as a part of a suite of Adobe products.
2 Choose **File, Open...**	To display the Open dialog box.
Select **Squash**	In the current topic folder.
Click **Open**	To open the image file named Tomatoes. You'll save the image in Photoshop format.
3 Choose **File, Save As...**	To open the Save As dialog box.
Edit the File name box to read **My squash**	File name: My squash
4 Observe the Format list	This is a JPEG file. You haven't added layers to it, so Photoshop prompts you to save it in its original file format.
From the Format list, select **Photoshop (*.PSD;*.PDD)**	JPEG (*.JPG;*.JPEG;*.JPE) Photoshop (*.PSD;*.PDD) Large Document Format (*.PSB) BMP (*.BMP;*.RLE;*.DIB) CompuServe GIF (*.GIF) Photoshop EPS (*.EPS) Photoshop DCS 1.0 (*.EPS) Photoshop DCS 2.0 (*.EPS) IFF Format (*.IFF;*.TDI) JPEG (*.JPG;*.JPEG;*.JPE) JPEG 2000 (*.JPF;*.JPX;*.JP2;*.J2C;*.J2K;*.JPC) JPEG Stereo (*.JPS) Multi-Picture Format (*.MPO) PCX (*.PCX) Photoshop PDF (*.PDF;*.PDP) Photoshop Raw (*.RAW) Pixar (*.PXR) PNG (*.PNG;*.PNS) Portable Bit Map (*.PBM;*.PGM;*.PPM;*.PNM;*.PFM;*.PAM) Scitex CT (*.SCT) Targa (*.TGA;*.VDA;*.ICB;*.VST) TIFF (*.TIF;*.TIFF) To save the image as a native Photoshop file.
5 Click **Save**	To save the image in the current topic folder.

The Save for Web dialog box

Explanation

When you're working with an image intended for display on the Web, you can save a copy of the image that is optimized for the Web. Images on the Web typically use the JPEG, GIF, or PNG format.

You should always keep a copy of your image in Photoshop format with all layers so you can return to it for any future modifications. Fortunately, the File, Save for Web command always saves a copy of the image in a new format, without replacing the original image. You don't have to flatten the original image layers before choosing the Save for Web command because it automatically flattens all layers in the copy of the image it generates.

To save an image for Web use:

1 Choose File, Save for Web to open the Save for Web dialog box. Shown in Exhibit 1-2.

2 From the Preset list, select a named collection of settings to optimize the image for Web use.

3 Specify any additional settings you want to use:

- If you want to customize the settings, select an option from the settings under Preset.

- If you want to adjust the image's pixel dimensions, specify the dimensions you want under Image Size. Press Tab.

- If you want to preview additional optimization settings, click the 4-Up tab, select one of the duplicate previews, and specify the optimization settings you want to use. Then select the preview with the settings you want to use.

4 Click Save to open the Save Optimized As dialog box. Enter a name in the Save As box, and click Save.

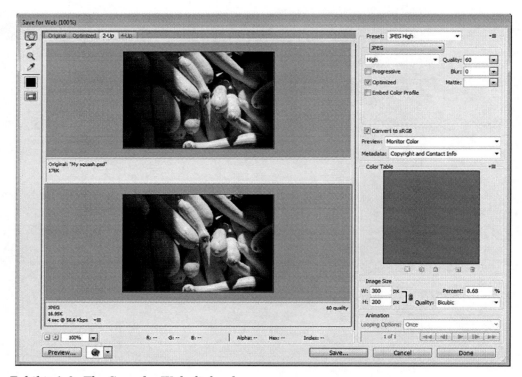

Exhibit 1-2: The Save for Web dialog box

In the Save for Web dialog box, you can specify the image format you want to use, such as GIF, JPEG, or PNG. You can also specify additional settings to optimize the image's appearance and file size. File size is important for Web images because smaller files will download over the Internet and load in a browser more quickly.

Do it!

A-2:   Saving an image for Web use

Here's how	Here's why
1 Choose **File**, **Save for Web...**	To open the Save for Web dialog box. You'll save it in the JPEG format.
2 From the Preset list, select **JPEG High**	Preset: JPEG High ▼
3 Under Image Size, edit the W box to read **300**	Image Size W: 300 px H: 200 px
	To set the width to 300 pixels. The height resizes proportionally.
Press (TAB)	To apply the new pixel dimensions. The preview updates to reflect the new dimensions.
4 In the left pane of the dialog box, click the **2-Up** tab	To preview both the original image and the optimized version.
Observe the file sizes	(Under each image.) The original file size is 176K, and the optimized file is much smaller.
5 Click **Save**	To open the Save Optimized As dialog box.
Name the image **squash_web**	
In the Save in list, navigate to the current topic folder	
Click **Save**	To save the image and return to the original version.
6 Choose **File**, **Save**	To update the original file.
Choose **File**, **Close**	

Topic B: The Photoshop environment

This topic covers the following ACE exam objectives for Photoshop CS6.

#	Objective
3.1	**Navigating the Photoshop workspace**
3.1.1	Zooming and moving around an image in Photoshop
3.1.2	Setting up guides, rulers, and grid units
3.1.3	Using keyboard shortcuts to temporarily select tools
3.1.4	Selecting, modifying, and replacing Photoshop workspace and keyboard shortcuts
3.1.5	Understanding the Application frame

Photoshop CS6

Explanation

Photoshop is a graphics-editing program for working with digital images and video. You might use Photoshop to enhance a digital photo; to transform objects in an image; to create an ad that includes photos, text, and other graphic elements; or to create original digital artwork. When you finish working with an image, you can save it in a format appropriate for Web, print, or video use.

Photoshop's environment provides great flexibility for viewing and editing images. You can use the Tools panel, the menu bar, the Options bar, panels, and other elements in their default arrangement, as shown in Exhibit 1-3, or you can customize their arrangement to suit your specific needs.

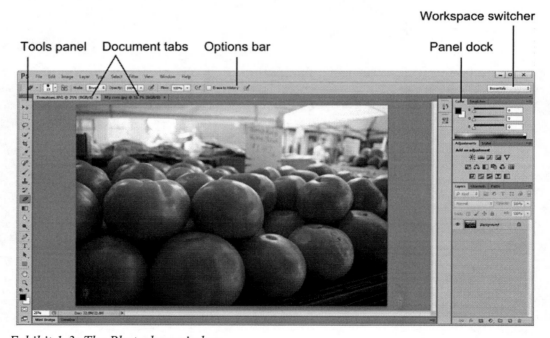

Exhibit 1-3: The Photoshop window

The following table describes the components of the Photoshop window.

Component	Function
Tools panel	Contains tools to select, draw, paint, edit, and view images. You can also choose foreground and background colors, create quick masks, and use tools to rotate, move, and zoom the image.
Document tabs	Display the name of the file you're working on, the current magnification, and the document's color mode. Can also be used to switch to other open files.
Options bar	Displays the various options and settings for a selected tool. The options vary depending on the active tool.
Panel dock	Contains panel groups, which display options and commands you can use to modify images. Panels can be docked or floating.
Workspace switcher	Contains options for displaying panels related to specific operations, such as motion, painting, photography, or typography. The Essentials workspace is the initial selection. Preset options are available, or you can save custom layouts.
Document statistics box	(At the bottom of the document window.) Displays data about the open image. Click the arrow next to the Document statistics box and select an option to choose the type of file data you want to show. You can show data such as the document size and profile.

Photoshop screen modes

While you're working with an image, you might want to temporarily hide panels or other Photoshop elements so you can focus on the image. You can do so by using the Change Screen Mode button, located at the bottom of the Tools panel. Click the button to cycle through screen modes, or click and hold the button to display a menu of screen modes, as shown in Exhibit 1-4. You can also use keyboard shortcuts to change the screen mode, or you can press F to cycle through the display options.

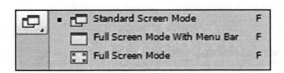

Exhibit 1-4: The Change Screen Mode menu

To hide and show window elements, use the techniques explained in the following table.

Technique	Used to...
From the Change Screen Mode menu, choose Standard Screen Mode	View the image in a document window and display the Tools panel and the panel dock.
From the Screen Mode menu, choose Full Screen Mode With Menu Bar	Expand the document window to fill the workspace, and make Photoshop occupy the full screen. The panels are still displayed.
From the Screen Mode menu, choose Full Screen Mode	Hide everything except the image, which is displayed on a black background. Press Esc or F to return to Standard Screen Mode.
Press Tab	Hide or show all panels, including the Options bar.
Press Shift+Tab	Hide or show all panels except the Options bar and the Tools panel.
Press Ctrl+Tab	Switch between different open documents.
Press F	Cycle through screen modes.

The Rotate View tool

Sometimes, the element you want to look at in an image might be at an odd angle, sideways, or upside down. You could rotate the image, but doing so would modify the image, which you might not want to do. Instead, you can use the Rotate View tool to change the image's orientation. Also, by using this tool, you can precisely control how the view is rotated.

To use the Rotate View tool, first select it in the Tools panel (the Rotate View tool is grouped with the Hand tool, so you might need to click and hold the Hand tool to see it). You can also press R to select the Rotate View tool. Then click and drag in the image to rotate the view. Or, on the Options bar, enter a number in the Rotation Angle box and press Enter to specify an exact angle.

OpenGL features

In order to speed up some functions and to display some interface elements, Photoshop can work with your computer's GPU (graphics processing unit). This works only if the GPU supports the OpenGL standard. Older hardware or operating systems might not support this function. To see if your system does, choose Edit, Preferences, Performance. If the settings in the GPU Settings panel are grayed out, your system doesn't support OpenGL. If it doesn't, you won't, for example, be able to use the Rotate View tool, as well as some other features.

The Application frame

In Windows, elements of the Photoshop interface always appear in an *application frame*. However, if you use a Mac operating system, you might be used to interface elements that appear as if they are floating over the desktop—this is now the default arrangement for Mac OS. To switch to the traditional, Windows-style application frame, you can choose Application Frame from the Window menu.

Do it!

B-1: Exploring the Photoshop window

The files for this activity are in Student Data folder **Unit 1\Topic B**.

Here's how	Here's why
1 Choose **File, Open…**	
Select **Tomatoes**	In the current topic folder.
Click **Open**	To open the image file named Tomatoes.
2 At the bottom of the Tools panel, click and hold 🖳	(The Change Screen Mode button.) To display a menu.
Choose **Full Screen Mode With Menu Bar**	To maximize the Photoshop window and make the image window fill the workspace.
3 Display the Change Screen Mode menu and choose **Full Screen Mode**	A message box appears.
Click **Full Screen**	To hide everything but the image.
4 Press F	To change to Standard Screen Mode.
5 Press TAB	To hide the panels and the Options bar.
Press TAB again	To show the panels and the Options bar.
Press SHIFT + TAB	To hide the panel dock.
Press SHIFT + TAB again	To show all of the panels.
6 Choose **File, Open…**	
Select **Corn** and click **Open**	To display another image in a tabbed window.
7 Choose **File**, **Save As…**	To open the Save As dialog box.
Navigate to the current topic folder	
Edit the File name box to read **My corn**	
Click **Save**	The JPEG Options dialog box appears.
Click **OK**	To save the file with the default settings.

8 Choose **Image**, **Image Rotation**, **90° CW**	To rotate the image. Doing so modifies the image. You can also rotate the view without rotating the image.
Press CTRL + Z	To undo the image rotation.
9 In the Tools panel, click and hold 🖐	To display the Hand tool and the Rotate View tool.
Select the **Rotate View Tool**	The Rotate View tool now replaces the Hand tool in the Tools panel.
Click and drag in the image	To rotate the view without changing the image.
Press and hold SHIFT and drag until the image appears upright	Holding Shift constrains the rotation to 15-degree increments.
10 Observe the document tab	It shows the document's name, the magnification setting, and image mode information.
11 Click as shown	(The document tab.) To select the first image.

Tomatoes.JPG @ 16.7% (RGB/8) ×   My corn.jpg @ 16.7% (RGB/8) ×

The Photoshop workspace

Explanation

The Photoshop *workspace* consists of the particular arrangement of panels that are currently displayed. If you regularly rearrange the panels for various workflows, you can save time by saving a particular arrangement of panels as a workspace. You can then load that workspace to automatically return to that panel arrangement.

To save a workspace:

1 Arrange the panels the way you want them.
2 On the Options bar, click the Workspace list button and choose New Workspace to open the New Workspace dialog box, shown in Exhibit 1-5.
3 Edit the Name box to identify the workspace.
4 Under Capture, specify the components you want to save as part of the workspace.
5 Click Save.

With the Live Workspace feature, you can make adjustments to the workspace and Photoshop will save them automatically. Then, if you switch to another workspace and then switch back, the panels will be configured as you left them previously.

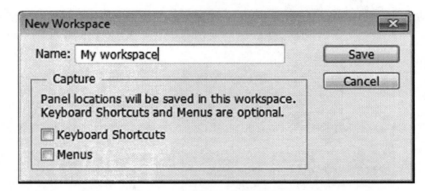

Exhibit 1-5: The New Workspace dialog box

To load a workspace, choose it from the Workspace list. To return a workspace to its default settings, choose Window, Workspace, Reset [Workspace name] or choose Reset [Workspace name] from the Workspace list.

To delete a workspace, choose Delete Workspace from the Workspace list. In the Delete Workspace dialog box, select the workspace you want to delete from the list, and click Delete. (Note, however, that you can't delete the active workspace.)

In addition to creating your own workspaces, you can use one of the default workspaces provided in Photoshop. To do so, click the Workspace list and select one of the preset workspaces. The workspace options are also available in the Window, Workspace submenu.

Panels

You probably won't need to use all of Photoshop's panels for any single image. You can open, close, and rearrange panels to best meet your needs. Open a panel by choosing it from the Window menu, and close a panel by clicking its menu button and choosing Close or Close Tab Group. Panels are placed by default in the panel dock, shown in Exhibit 1-6, on the right side of the application window.

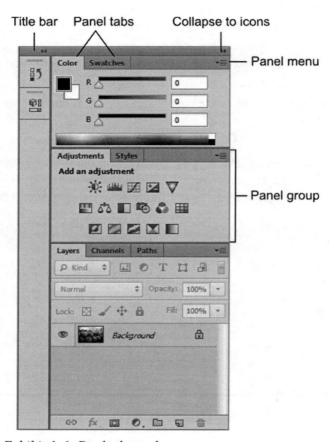

Exhibit 1-6: Docked panels

When a panel dock is collapsed, it displays icons for the available panels. To collapse the entire dock, click the Collapse to Icons button in the top-right corner of the dock. Alternatively, you can click individual icons to show only the desired panels (as well as any others contained in the panel group), as shown in Exhibit 1-7.

You can drag a panel's tab away from the panel group to remove the panel from the group and make it a floating panel. And you can drag a panel's tab next to the other tabs in a panel group to add that panel to the group. In addition, you can drag panel tabs to and from the docks, or you can create a new dock and add the panels you want to it. To do so, drag a panel's tab to the side of an existing dock until a blue line appears around the group; then release the mouse button.

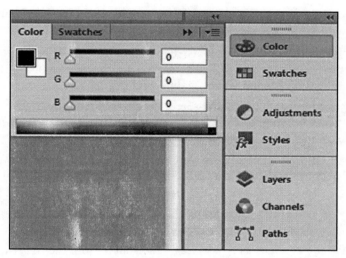

Exhibit 1-7: A collapsed panel dock with a panel group expanded

The Tools panel

The Tools panel provides various tools used to work with images. Some tools are visible, and some are hidden. A small triangle in the lower-right corner of a tool's button indicates that hidden tools are available. To display them, either click and hold the tool until a tool list appears, or right-click the tool. In the list, the selected tool is marked with a black square. You can select another tool by clicking its name in the list. Additionally, most tools have a single-letter keyboard shortcut associated with them.

Customizing shortcuts and menus

Photoshop provides keyboard shortcuts that you can use to quickly select a tool, menu, or operation. For instance, to undo a change, you can press Ctrl+Z rather than choosing Edit, Undo. For commands with keyboard shortcuts, the shortcut is displayed in the menu. Likewise, in the Tools panel, the flyout menu for tool groups shows keyboard shortcuts for selecting tools.

You can change shortcuts and create shortcuts by using the Keyboard Shortcuts and Menus dialog box. To create a shortcut:

1 Choose Edit, Keyboard Shortcuts.

2 From the Shortcuts For list, select the appropriate category. Choices include Application Menus, Panel Menus, and Tools.

3 Expand the categories and select the desired command. Then enter or change the key combination and click Accept. If the combination is already assigned, you are offered two options:

- Click Accept and Go To Conflict to specify a new shortcut for the current command and then to choose a new shortcut for the command that the shortcut was previously used for.

- Click Undo Changes to cancel the new shortcut. You can then try a different key combination.

4 Save the changes as a new set of shortcuts. From the Set list, you can select your custom set or select Photoshop Defaults. Before saving a set, you can discard any changes by clicking Cancel.

You can customize the display of menus by using the Menus tab in the Keyboard Shortcuts and Menus dialog box. Many, though not all, menu items can be hidden in order to simplify menus and display only commands you commonly use. You can apply colors to commands to make them stand out or to enable color-coded instructions.

To customize menus:

1 Choose Edit, Menus.

2 From the Menu For list, select either Application Menus or Panel Menus.

3 Expand the menu categories.

4 Click the button in the Visibility column to hide an item.

5 In the Color column, click None and select a color.

6 Save the customized menus as a new set.

There are two ways to display hidden menu items:

- Press Ctrl before you click the menu.

- Choose Show All Menu Items at the bottom of the menu.

You can turn off the menu colors by clearing Show Menu Colors in the Interface section of the Preferences dialog box.

Do it!

B-2: Organizing the workspace

Here's how	Here's why
1 Click the **Channels** panel tab	(In the Layers panel group.) You'll undock Channels to make it a floating panel.
Drag the Channels panel tab to the left as shown	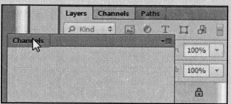
	Until the Channel panel separates from the dock.
Drag the Channels panel into the document window	So that it doesn't overlap the panel dock.
2 Choose **Window**, **History**	To display the History panel. In the default Essentials workspace, the History panel is in the panel dock.
3 Drag the **History** panel tab to the Channels panel	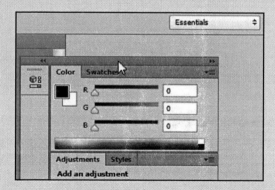
	To remove the History panel from the dock and create a new panel group.
4 Drag the Color panel group's title bar, as shown, into the document window	
	To undock the panels.
5 Click the Collapse to Icons button, as shown	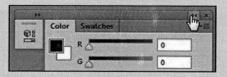
	To collapse the dock.
	Now that you have the workspace arranged in a particular way, you will save it so that you can use it at any time.

6 On the Options bar, click **Essentials ⬍**	(The Workspace switcher.) To show a menu of workspace options.
Choose **New Workspace...**	To open the New Workspace dialog box.
Edit the Name box to read **My workspace**	
Click **Save**	To save the workspace.
7 Drag the Color panel group to the right side of the document window	Drag it close to the edge of the application frame, but don't dock it.
8 Drag the History panel group below the Color panel group, as shown	
	Photoshop's Live Workspace feature will retain the positions of the panels.
9 Click the Workspace list and choose **Essentials**	To return to the Essentials workspace. The live workspace feature has remembered the positions the panels were in before you saved the new workspace.
10 Click the Workspace list and choose **Reset Essentials**	To return the workspace to its default settings.

Magnification and scrolling techniques

Explanation

When you're working with an image, you'll often need to zoom in closely to see and adjust small details. You'll then need to zoom back out to see the entire image.

The following table describes techniques for changing image magnification.

Zoom technique/tool	Description
Zoom tool	Select the Zoom tool; then click the image to zoom in, or drag over part of an image to zoom in on that area. Press Alt and click to zoom out. As you adjust the magnification, the document window's size remains unchanged. To adjust the window size as you zoom, check Resize Windows to Fit on the options bar.
Temporarily accessing the Zoom tool	When you're using any tool, press Ctrl+Spacebar to access the Zoom tool, or press Alt+Spacebar to access the Zoom Out tool.
View commands	From the View menu, choose commands to zoom in, zoom out, fit the image in the available space, view the image at 100%, or view the image at the approximate print size. Most of these commands have corresponding keyboard shortcuts, shown in the menu.
Navigator panel	At the bottom of the Navigator panel, click the Zoom In or Zoom Out buttons, drag the Zoom slider, or enter a value in the Zoom box.
Zoom box	(At the bottom of the document window.) Edit the value to change the image's magnification.

When you display an image at 100% magnification, one screen pixel is used to display one image pixel, giving you the most accurate view of the image. At 200% magnification, two screen pixels re-create each image pixel; and at 50% magnification, one screen pixel is forced to display two image pixels. In either case, the image is somewhat distorted. To display an image at 100% magnification, choose View, Actual Pixels. To view an image at the size at which it will print, choose View, Print Size.

Scrolling an image

When you zoom in on an image, you might need to scroll to see different parts of it. You can drag the window's scrollbars, but a more intuitive method is to pan by using the Hand tool to drag the image. You can select the Hand tool from the Tools panel, or you can select it temporarily by pressing Spacebar. In addition, in the Navigator panel, you can drag the proxy preview area, shown in Exhibit 1-8, to pan the image.

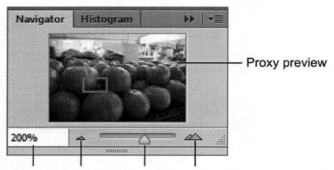

Exhibit 1-8: The Navigator panel

Temporary tool selection

By default, most tools are assigned a single-letter keyboard shortcut. For example, to select the Hand tool, you could press H. However, sometimes you only want to use a tool temporarily and then switch back to the tool you were using. To do this, press and hold the tool's keyboard shortcut, and then click or drag in the image to use that tool. When you're finished, release the key to return the previously selected tool.

The following are keyboard shortcuts for temporarily selecting tools to magnify and scroll an image:

- **Spacebar** – Press to temporarily select the Hand tool.
- **Ctrl+Spacebar** – Press to temporarily select the Zoom In tool.
- **Alt+Spacebar** – Press to temporarily select the Zoom Out tool.

Do it!

B-3: Magnifying and scrolling images

Here's how	Here's why
1 Verify that the Tomatoes document window is active	Click its tab, if necessary.
Press and hold CTRL + SPACEBAR	To temporarily access the Zoom In tool. (Continue pressing and holding Ctrl+Spacebar throughout this step.)
Click the document	To zoom in one level of magnification.
Click in the center of the image and drag right	(Drag until the tomatoes fill the document window.) The Scrubby Zoom feature enables you to zoom in a freeform manner. Dragging left would zoom out again.
Release CTRL + SPACEBAR	To return to the selected tool.
2 Press and hold ALT + SPACEBAR and click anywhere in the image	To zoom out one level of magnification.
Release ALT + SPACEBAR	
3 In the Tools panel, click 🔍	To select the Zoom tool.
Press and hold ALT, and click three times	To zoom out, decreasing image magnification.
Release ALT, and click twice	To zoom in again.
4 Choose **View, Fit on Screen**	
At the bottom-left of the document window, observe the magnification	32.94% 🕒 The magnification percentage is not a whole number.
5 Zoom in to 200% magnification	(Click with the Zoom tool.) When you're viewing a magnified image, you often can't see the entire image in the window. Although you can use scrollbars, it's often easier to use the Hand tool to pan the image. As with the Zoom tool, you can access the Hand tool temporarily.

6 Press and hold `SPACEBAR`	To temporarily access the Hand tool.
Drag from the center of the image to the right	(Continue to press the Spacebar while dragging.) To view the image area that was previously beyond the left edge of the window.
When the mouse pointer is at the right edge of the window, release the mouse button and then release `SPACEBAR`	The image is not distorted, but it is slightly jagged because each image pixel is now represented by a 2 pixel × 2 pixel block.
	When you zoom in so closely, it's sometimes difficult to know what part of the image you're looking at. You can use the Navigator panel to see the whole image.
7 Choose **Window, Navigator**	To open the Navigator panel group.
Click once as shown	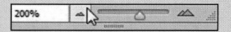
	To zoom out to 100%.
In the Navigator panel, drag the proxy preview area	
	To pan to different parts of the image.
In the Navigator panel, click ▶▶	To hide the panel.
8 Close Tomatoes	Choose File, Close. If asked to save changes, click No.
Click as shown	**My corn.jpg @ 16.7% (RGB/8)** ☒
	To close My corn.

Guides, rulers, and grids

Explanation   Rulers aren't shown by default in Photoshop, but they can be a big help when working with an image. To display the rulers, choose View, Rulers or press Ctrl+R.

When the horizontal and vertical rulers are displayed, you can create guides to more easily align image elements or visualize a layout. To add a guide, drag from either ruler; when you release the mouse button in the image window, a blue line appears. To move guides, select the Move tool and drag them. To remove a guide from an image, drag the guide back to the ruler; to remove all guides from an image, choose View, Clear Guides.

You can position a guide precisely by choosing View, New Guide to open the New Guide dialog box. Select either Horizontal or Vertical, enter the desired position, and click OK.

You can also specify properties for guides. To do so, choose Edit, Preferences, Guides, Grid & Slices. In the Preferences dialog box, specify settings for guides and click OK.

Finally, you can specify how guides snap to objects in an image:

- To snap a guide to ruler ticks, press Shift as you drag the guide.
- To have objects snap to guides as you drag the object, choose View, Snap To, Guides.
- To prevent a guide from snapping to objects as you drag it, hold Ctrl.

To hide guides, choose View, Show, Guides to clear the selection in the menu, or press Ctrl+; (Ctrl + semi-colon). To lock guides so they can't be moved, choose View, Lock Guides.

Smart guides

Smart Guides can help you position elements such as shapes, layers, and selections. To view them, choose View, Show, Smart Guides. At first, you might not notice a difference—that's because Smart Guides only appear when you're moving an object or selection and it interacts with the edge of another image element.

Grids

A grid can be useful when arranging elements horizontally and vertically, especially when symmetry is important. To show the grid, choose View, Show, Grid. The default spacing is 1" squares with four subdivisions, as shown in Exhibit 1-9. You can adjust this, as well as other settings for guides and rulers, by choosing Edit, Preferences, Guides, Grid & Slices.

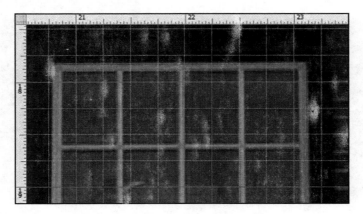

Exhibit 1-9: Default grid spacing and coloring

Do it!

B-4: Setting up guides, rulers, and grids

The files for this activity are in Student Data folder **Unit 1\Topic B**.

Here's how	Here's why
1 Choose **File, Open…**	
Choose **City market**	In the current topic folder.
Click **Open**	
2 Choose **View, Rulers**	(Or press Ctrl+R.) To display the horizontal and vertical rulers.
3 Point to the horizontal ruler, click, and drag down	To create a horizontal ruler guide.
Drag the guide to the indicated position	You can use ruler guides to align objects with elements in images.
4 Choose **View, Show, Grid**	To display gridlines. You want the gridlines to align roughly with the windows in the building.
5 Zoom in on the top-center window	In addition to the spacing, you'll adjust the color so that you can more easily distinguish the gridlines from the lines in the image.

6 Point to the indicated area

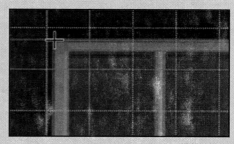

You can adjust the origin point of the ruler by dragging from here into the image.

Drag as shown

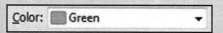

To change the ruler's origin point to the top-left of the window.

7 Choose **Edit, Preferences, Guides, Grid & Slices**

To open the Preferences dialog box.

Under Grid, from the Color list, select **Green**

Color: Green   ▾

In the image, the gridlines change to green.

Edit the Gridline every box to read **2.4**

To align the 1" gridlines with the sides of the window. Because the gridlines update as soon as you adjust their settings, you can enter values until you get a close match.

Because the window also is divided into four vertical sections, you won't change the Subdivisions value.

Click **OK**

8 Choose **View, Show, Grid**

To hide the gridlines.

9 Close the image

If asked to save changes, click No.

Topic C: Tool options and presets

This topic covers the following ACE exam objectives for Photoshop CS6.

#	Objective
3.2	**Importing and exporting presets**
3.2.1	Knowing the location of preset files on both a PC and Mac platform
3.2.2	Understanding the process of exporting and importing presets
3.3	**Resetting sliders and options**
3.3.1	Working with sliders and buttons
3.3.2	Using Alt key combinations
3.3.3	Resetting parameters
3.3.4	Using Shift modifiers
3.4	**Using tool groups and options**
3.4.2	Modifying individual tool options
3.4.3	Creating tool presets

The Preset Manager

Explanation

The brushes, swatches, gradients, styles, patterns, contours, custom shapes, and tools you'll use in Photoshop each have several sets of predefined settings that are stored as *presets*. You can access presets from the option bar and from various panels, and you can modify presets, create your own, and import other presets.

You can use the Preset Manager dialog box to load presets that come with Photoshop. You can also use the Preset Manager dialog box to save a group of presets you've created or edited. The group is saved as a file called a *set*. Sets can be useful for a few reasons:

- You can share sets of presets with other people for consistency.
- You can create multiple preset files that you can load for different purposes (for example, a designer could save different color panels for different clients).
- If you need to reinstall Photoshop, you can reload the presets you saved instead of losing them.

To manage presets and sets:

1   Choose Edit, Presets, Preset Manager (or choose Preset Manager from a panel menu) to open the Preset Manager dialog box, shown in Exhibit 1-10.

2   From the Preset Type list, select one of the eight preset types.

3   Select the presets you want to work with. Shift+click to select a range of adjacent presets, or Ctrl+click to select non-adjacent ones.

4   Click Save Set to save the selected presets as a set. If you save the set in the default location (a subfolder of the Presets folder within the Photoshop application folder), then after you close and re-open Photoshop, the set will appear in the relevant panel menu (or in the Tool Preset picker), along with sets that came with Photoshop.

Exhibit 1-10: The Preset Manager dialog box

Tool presets

Many tools have several presets from which you can select. You can also use tool presets to save and reuse your own settings for a particular tool.

To create a tool preset:

1   Select the tool for which you want to create a preset.

2   On the options bar, specify the tool settings you want to store as a preset.

3   Do either of the following to open the New Tool Preset dialog box:

    • On the left side of the options bar, click the Tool Preset icon to display the Tool Preset picker, and click the "Create new tool preset" icon.

    • Choose Window, Tool Presets to open the Tool Presets panel, shown in Exhibit 1-11, and click the "Create new tool preset" icon.

4   In the New Tool Preset dialog box, enter a name for the preset and click OK.

After saving a tool preset, you can select it from the Tool Preset picker or from the Tool Presets panel. If you want to reset the current tool to its default settings, then right-click the Tool Preset icon on the options bar and choose Reset Tool.

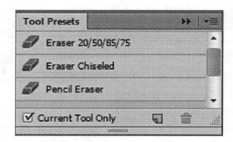

Exhibit 1-11: The Tool Presets panel

Tool options

When you select a tool, the options bar automatically updates to display that tool's options, as shown in Exhibit 1-12. Sometimes, the tool's default options might be enough to accomplish your task. However, there are many cases in which you'll want to modify these options so that the tool is better suited to your needs.

To modify options for a tool, select it so that the options bar displays its options. Then use the drop-down lists, boxes, sliders, and other settings to modify the tool's behavior.

Exhibit 1-12: Options for the Eraser tool

Sometimes, when dragging a slider or editing a value on the options bar, it's difficult to observe the change to the image you're editing at the same time. You can use keyboard shortcuts to change these settings so that you don't need to take your eye from the image. To do so, place the insertion point in a box on the options slider and press Up Arrow or Down Arrow to modify a setting incrementally by a value of 1. If a slider is displayed, you also can press Left Arrow or Right Arrow to modify the value.

If a brush or painting tool is selected, you can also use the Left Bracket and Right Bracket keys to decrease or increase brush size in increments of 5.

If you press Shift while pressing an arrow key to modify a value, the value changes by a factor of 10. For example, if the value is 53, then pressing Shift+Down Arrow (if the insertion point is in the box) will change it to 43.

To reset a tool's options to their default settings, on the options bar, right-click the Tool Preset picker and choose Reset Tool. You can also choose Reset All Tools to reset every tool in Photoshop to its default values.

Scrubby sliders

In most cases, if a setting has a box in which you can enter a value and a drop-down slider, you can also change the setting's value by pointing to that setting's name or formatting icon and dragging left or right. This is called *scrubbing*, and as you scrub, the values you select are applied to the selected or active element in the image. Scrubbing is useful for applying formatting values visually (you can see the effects of the changes as you make them).

Resetting dialog box settings

The Alt key has a number of functions in Photoshop. When you press it while using a
selection tool, for example, it modifies the selection marquee. It also modifies other
commands; holding Alt while clicking the "Create a new layer" button, for example,
opens a dialog box that would otherwise not open. But the Alt key can also be used
while viewing a dialog box to reset parameters. For example, if you've entered values in
a dialog box and want to return to the default values, pressing Alt changes the dialog
box's Cancel button to a Reset button.

Do it!

C-1:   **Creating a tool preset**

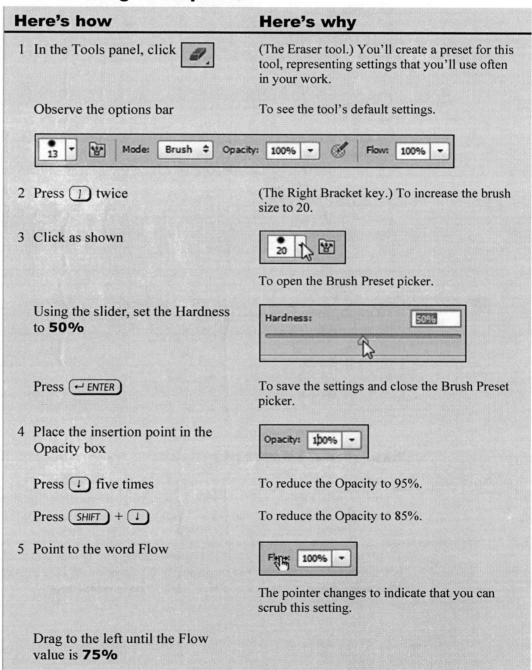

Here's how	Here's why
1 In the Tools panel, click	(The Eraser tool.) You'll create a preset for this tool, representing settings that you'll use often in your work.
Observe the options bar	To see the tool's default settings.
2 Press ⌷ twice	(The Right Bracket key.) To increase the brush size to 20.
3 Click as shown	To open the Brush Preset picker.
Using the slider, set the Hardness to **50%**	
Press ↵ ENTER	To save the settings and close the Brush Preset picker.
4 Place the insertion point in the Opacity box	
Press ↓ five times	To reduce the Opacity to 95%.
Press SHIFT + ↓	To reduce the Opacity to 85%.
5 Point to the word Flow	The pointer changes to indicate that you can scrub this setting.
Drag to the left until the Flow value is **75%**	

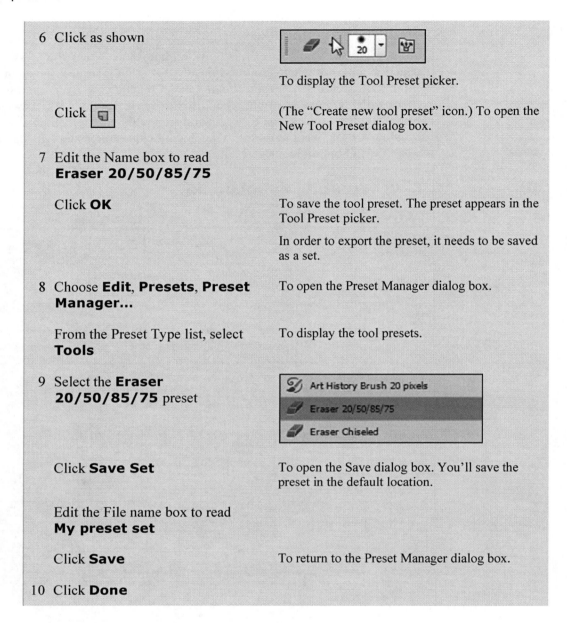

6 Click as shown

To display the Tool Preset picker.

Click (The "Create new tool preset" icon.) To open the New Tool Preset dialog box.

7 Edit the Name box to read **Eraser 20/50/85/75**

Click **OK** To save the tool preset. The preset appears in the Tool Preset picker.

In order to export the preset, it needs to be saved as a set.

8 Choose **Edit, Presets, Preset Manager...** To open the Preset Manager dialog box.

From the Preset Type list, select **Tools** To display the tool presets.

9 Select the **Eraser 20/50/85/75** preset

Click **Save Set** To open the Save dialog box. You'll save the preset in the default location.

Edit the File name box to read **My preset set**

Click **Save** To return to the Preset Manager dialog box.

10 Click **Done**

Export and import of presets

Explanation In order to export presets you've created, they need to be saved as part of a set. To export presets, choose Edit, Presets, Export/Import Presets to open the Export/Import presets dialog box. Select the presets you want to export and click the add icon to add them to the list of presets to export. Then click Export Presets.

To import a presets file, open the Export/Import dialog box and click the Import Presets tab. Click Select Import Folder to specify the location of your preset files. Select the presets to import, click the add icon, then click Import Presets.

Location of preset files

When you create presets, they're saved, by default, separately from the presets that are included with Photoshop. In Windows 7, they're saved in the following location:

- [Drive]:\Users\<User>\AppData\Roaming\Adobe\Adobe Photoshop CS6\Presets

If you're using a Mac, presets are saved in the following location:

- <User>/Library/Application Support/Adobe/Adobe Photoshop CS6/Presets

Do it!

C-2: Exporting a preset

Here's how	Here's why
1 Choose **Edit, Presets, Export/Import Presets…**	To open the Export/Import Presets dialog box.
Under Your Presets, select **(Tools) My preset set.tpl**	
Click >	To add it to the Presets to Export list.
2 Click **Export Presets**	At the bottom of the dialog box.
Navigate to the current topic folder	
Click **OK**	A message box indicates the set has been exported.
Click **OK**	
3 On the options bar, right-click as shown	
	(On the Tool Preset picker.) To display a shortcut menu.
Choose **Reset Tool**	To return the tool settings to the defaults.
4 Display the Tool Preset picker	You'll delete the preset you created.
Right-click **Eraser 20/50/85/75** and choose **Delete Tool Preset**	

Unit summary: Getting started

Topic A   In this unit, you learned about using different **file types** in Photoshop. Then you saved an image in **Photoshop format**. You also optimized an image in **JPEG format** for Web use.

Topic B   In this topic, you learned about the Photoshop environment, and you learned how to switch **screen modes**. You also arranged **panels** and saved a panel arrangement as a workspace. In addition, you learned how to **magnify** an image and scroll to view different parts of an image. Finally, you learned how to set up **rulers**, **guides**, and **grids**.

Topic C   In this unit, you learned how to specify **tool options**. Then you created and exported a **tool preset**.

Independent practice activity

In this activity, you'll open an image and save it in a format appropriate for print use. Then you'll adjust magnification, scroll, and create and save a custom workspace. Finally, you'll create a tool preset.

The files for this activity are in Student Data folder **Unit 1\Unit summary**.

1 Open the Apples 1 image.

2 Save the image as **My apples 1** in TIFF format. Use the default settings.

3 Fit the image on the screen.

4 Use Scrubby Zoom to zoom in on one of the apple stickers.

5 Use the Navigator panel to pan around the image.

6 Create an arrangement of panels that you like.

7 Save the arrangement as **My practice workspace**.

8 Switch to the Essentials workspace. Then reset the workspace.

9 Delete all custom workspaces.

10 Create a new preset for the Rectangular Marquee tool. Specify the Style option to be **Fixed Size**, and specify a size.

11 Delete the tool preset you created.

12 Update and close the image.

Review questions

1 Which image types are commonly used for Web applications?

   A JPEG.

   B GIF.

   C PNG.

   D All of the above.

2 When you zoom to 100% magnification, you see:

   A The image at the size it will be when printed

   B The image at a size that fills the monitor

   C One image pixel for each monitor pixel

   D The image at a size that fills its window

3 You've opened several panels and have arranged them in a way that works best for your workflow. How can you save this arrangement?

4 What key or key combination can you use to temporarily access the Zoom tool?

   A Ctrl+Spacebar

   B Alt+Spacebar

   C Spacebar

   D Ctrl+Alt+Spacebar

5 What key or key combination can you use to temporarily access the Hand tool?

   A Ctrl+Spacebar

   B Alt+Spacebar

   C Spacebar

   D Ctrl+Alt+Spacebar

6 You've adjusted the options for a number of tools but now want to return them all to their defaults. How do you do so?

   A In the Tool Preset picker, right-click any presets and choose Delete Tool Preset.

   B In the Tool Presets panel, right-click any presets and choose Delete Tool Preset.

   C On the options bar, right-click the Tool Preset picker and choose Reset Tool.

   D On the options bar, right-click the Tool Preset picker and choose Reset All Tools.

7 You've created a tool preset, but it isn't appearing in the Export/Import Presets dialog box. What do you need to do?

Unit 2

Image selections

Complete this unit, and you'll know how to:

A Use various tools to select image areas.

B Modify and manipulate selections.

Topic A: Selection techniques

This topic covers the following ACE exam objectives for Photoshop CS6.

#	Objective
3.4	**Using tool groups and options**
3.4.1	Selecting tools from a tool group
4.1	**Creating selections using appropriate tools**
4.1.1	Creating selections with various tools and determining which selection tools work best for a given situation
4.1.2	Working with the Quick Selection tool and options

Selection tools

Explanation

If you want to manipulate or modify just a portion of an image, you'll have to select that portion. After you select the part of the image you want to work with, you can move it, change its color attributes, or apply any number of effects to it.

The technique you use to select part of an image will depend on the attributes of the area you want to select. The following table lists several Photoshop selection tools, along with the type of image areas each tool is best suited to select.

Selection tool	Icon	Description
Rectangular Marquee		Selects square or rectangular areas.
Elliptical Marquee		Selects circular or elliptical areas.
Single Row Marquee		Selects a single row of pixels.
Single Column Marquee		Selects a single column of pixels.
Lasso		Selects irregularly shaped, curving areas.
Polygonal Lasso		Selects irregularly shaped areas made up of straight lines.
Magnetic Lasso		Selects areas that have edges that contrast with the abutting area.
Quick Selection		Automatically detects and selects areas based on defined edges in the image.
Magic Wand		Selects areas that contrast with other image areas.

The marquee tools

You can select rectangular or elliptical areas by dragging the Rectangular Marquee tool or the Elliptical Marquee tool, respectively. After you drag to create a selection, a marquee appears around it. (This animated marquee is sometimes referred to as "marching ants" because of its appearance.) By default, the pointer for the marquee tools appears as a cross. However, if you point inside the selection with one of the marquee tools, the pointer changes to a white arrowhead next to a dotted rectangle, indicating that you can drag to move the selection. When a selection tool is selected, you can also press the arrow keys to move the marquee in small increments.

You can press a modifier key to change how the Rectangular and Elliptical Marquee tools work, as follows:

- To constrain a selection to a perfect square or circle, press Shift as you drag.
- To select from the center outward, press Alt as you drag.
- To move the marquee as you create it, press Spacebar as you drag.

After you select an area, you can apply commands that affect only the pixels inside the selection. If you want to apply a command to the entire image, you need to deselect the selection. To do so, choose Select, Deselect. If you find yourself deselecting often while you work, you might want to use the keyboard shortcut, Ctrl+D.

Additionally, if you need to select a row or column only one-pixel wide (the smallest possible selection), you can use the Single Row Marquee and Single Column Marquee tools.

Hiding selection edges

After you make a selection, a selection marquee appears along its edge. The selection marquee obscures your view of the selection's edges, but it's often important to see the edges to ensure that the selection is accurate. If the selection isn't accurate, any work you perform on it might look sloppy. For example, if you select a fish from an image in which the water is dark blue and you move it to an image in which the water is light blue, a rough selection will make it obvious that the fish came from another image. To hide or show the selection marquee, choose View, Extras or press Ctrl+H.

Anti-aliasing

By default, each selection tool uses *anti-aliasing*, which softens a selection's edges by applying varying levels of transparency to the pixels along those edges. If you don't use anti-aliasing, then when you move a selection to another image, for example, the edges of the selection might appear jagged over the new background. If you want to turn off anti-aliasing for a selection tool, you can clear Anti-alias on the options bar.

Tool groups

With the exception of the Move tool and the Zoom tool, every tool in Photoshop is part of a tool group. To select the tool currently visible in the Tools panel, simply click it. You also can use the tool's keyboard shortcut—for example, if the Rectangular Marquee tool is visible in the Tools panel, press M to select it. But if you want to select a tool that isn't currently visible in the Tools panel, use one of the following options:

- Click and hold on the tool group to display a menu, then select the desired tool.
- Press Shift and the tool's keyboard shortcut. For example, to cycle between the tools in the marquee tool group, press Shift+M.
- Press Alt and click the tool group to cycle through the tools.

Do it!

A-1: Selecting rectangular and elliptical areas

The files for this activity are in Student Data folder **Unit 2\Topic A**.

Here's how	Here's why
1 Open Corn 1	(Choose File, Open.) You'll test to see whether selections from an image would be appropriate in another design.
2 Choose **File, Save As...**	
Edit the File name box to read **My corn 1**	
From the Format list, select **Photoshop (*.PSD;*.PDD)**	
Click **Save**	
3 Press `CTRL` + `O`	To fit the image on the screen.
4 In the Tools panel, click [⬚]	To select the Rectangular Marquee tool.
Under Style, choose **Normal**	If necessary.
Click in the center of the image and begin dragging down and to the right	Sometimes it's difficult to tell where to begin a selection, and you might want to change the selection marquee's position without starting over. You can move the selection marquee as you're making the selection.
Press `SPACEBAR`	While holding the mouse button to maintain the selection marquee.
Drag the selection marquee as shown	
	Move it to the top-left of the left ear of corn.

5 Release (SPACEBAR)	Without releasing the mouse button, to continue making the selection.
Drag down and to the right	To surround the ear of corn with a selection marquee. You could copy this selection and paste it into another image.
Release the mouse button	Next, you'll move the selection marquee. This method is useful if you want to make two selections that are exactly the same size. You could select the first area, copy and paste it into another image, and then move the selection marquee to another area in the original image and copy and paste it as well.
6 Point inside the marquee as shown	
	The pointer changes to indicate that you can now drag to move the marquee.
Drag the marquee to the right	To select the ear of corn on the right.
7 Press (CTRL) + (D)	To deselect the selection.
8 Choose **File, Save**	To update the image.
Press (CTRL) + (W)	To close the image.
9 Open Cabbage 1	
Save the image in Photoshop format as **My cabbage 1**	
10 Press (CTRL) + (0)	
11 In the Tools panel, click and hold [marquee icon]	To display the other marquee tools.
From the marquee tool group, select the **Elliptical Marquee Tool**	The Elliptical Marquee tool now replaces the Rectangular Marquee tool in the Tools panel. You'll draw an elliptical marquee around one of the heads of lettuce.

12 Point above and to the left of the topmost head of lettuce	
Drag down and to the right	(Press Spacebar while making the selection, if necessary.) To surround the lettuce with an elliptical selection marquee.
	You can often make a more precise selection with an elliptical marquee if you create the marquee from the center of the selection.
Deselect the selected area	Press Ctrl+D.
13 Point to the center of the head of lettuce	
Press and hold (ALT), and drag down and to the right	To create an elliptical marquee around the lettuce. The marquee forms from the center.
While still pressing the mouse button and (ALT), press (SPACEBAR) and drag	To move the marquee while you're creating it. Release Spacebar and drag if you want to continue adjusting the marquee size.
Press (ALT) and release (SPACEBAR) and drag	(As necessary.) To finish drawing the elliptical marquee around the head of lettuce.
14 Deselect the selected area	Press Ctrl+D.
Press (CTRL) + (S)	To update the image.

The Lasso tool

Explanation

You can use the Lasso tool to select irregularly shaped areas. To select an area of any shape, select the Lasso tool and drag in one continuous motion along the border of the area you want to select. When you release the mouse, Photoshop will automatically connect the ending point with the starting point to complete the selection.

When making a selection with the Lasso tool, you might also want to draw a straight line as part of the selection. You can combine the freehand selection and straight-edged segments by doing the following:

1   With the Lasso tool selected, begin making a freehand selection.

2   When you want to begin a straight-edged segment, press Alt and release the mouse button to temporarily select the Polygonal Lasso tool.

3   While holding Alt, point to where you want the straight-edged segment to end.

4   Click and hold the mouse button to complete the straight-edged segment.

5   Release Alt (while holding the mouse button) to continue drawing with the Lasso tool.

This is also a good technique to use if you need to pick up your mouse while you're making a selection—for example, if you're drawing with the Lasso tool and you reach the bottom of your mouse pad but need to draw farther down in the image. Press Alt, release the mouse button and reposition it on the mouse pad, click and hold the mouse button, and then release Alt and continue drawing the selection.

The Polygonal Lasso tool

If you need to select an irregularly shaped area that is made up of straight lines, you can use the Polygonal Lasso tool.

To select an image area by using the Polygonal Lasso tool:

1   With the Polygonal Lasso tool selected, click where you want to begin.

2   Point to the end of the first straight segment you want to select, and click.

3   Continue to click at the end of each straight area.

4   When you're finished, point to the spot you first clicked and click to complete the selection. You can also double-click and Photoshop will complete the selection automatically.

Just as you can select the Polygonal Lasso tool temporarily while using the Lasso tool, you can also temporarily select the Lasso tool while using the Polygonal Lasso tool. To do so, press Alt and drag. Release either Alt or the mouse button to return to the Polygonal Lasso tool.

The Magnetic Lasso tool

You can select irregularly shaped image areas with the Magnetic Lasso tool, similar to the way you'd use the Lasso tool. As you drag with the Magnetic Lasso tool, however, the selection snaps to areas where it detects high contrast. This tool is useful for selecting image areas with complex or irregular edges that contrast significantly with other areas.

As you move the Magnetic Lasso tool through an image to make a selection, points appear along the path you're creating. These points determine the path's shape. There are several ways to control the points added by the Magnetic Lasso tool:

• Click to specify the first point.

• Move the pointer along the area you want to select, and the Magnetic Lasso automatically adds points to generate the path.

• To force the path to continue through a specific location, click to add a point.

• If the most recent point appears where you don't want one, press Delete or Backspace to remove it.

• To remove all points and start over, press Esc.

The Magnetic Lasso tool adds points where it detects the highest contrast within a specified distance around the pointer. By default, the Magnetic Lasso tool operates within a distance of 10 pixels from the pointer. If you want the tool to examine a larger or smaller area around the pointer, you can change the value in the Width box on the options bar. In addition, you can press Caps Lock to display the pointer as a circle that shows the Width area, and you can press [or] to decrease or increase the Width value.

You can use the Contrast box to specify how much contrast must exist for the Magnetic Lasso tool to define a path. The higher the Contrast value, the greater the contrast must be for the Magnetic Lasso to define a path. In addition, you can adjust the value in the Frequency box to control how often points are added to define the path.

Finally, you can select the Lasso tool and the Polygonal Lasso tool while using the Magnetic Lasso tool. Press Alt and drag to temporarily select the Lasso tool, or press Alt and click to temporarily select the Polygonal Lasso tool.

A-2: Selecting with the Lasso tool

Here's how	Here's why
1 In the Tools panel, click	(The Lasso tool.) You'll use the Lasso tool to select the heads of lettuce.
2 Create a horizontal ruler guide as shown	

	(At about the 44.7" mark.) You'll use this to guide your selection.
3 Point to the top of the topmost head of lettuce	
Drag to the right around the edge of the lettuces	If you need to reposition the mouse while making the selection, then press Alt, move the mouse, click and hold the mouse, release Alt, and continue drawing the selection.
4 Drag to the right edge of the image	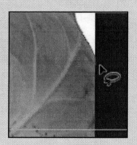
	When the Lasso tool gets to the edge of an image, it automatically follows the image boundary when you drag outside of it.
Drag outside the image area as shown	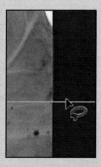
	To make the selection follow the image's edge.

5 Hold ⟨ALT⟩ and release the mouse   To temporarily select the Polygonal Lasso tool.

Point to the ruler guide at the left
edge of the image, click and hold
the mouse, and release ⟨ALT⟩   To continue the selection straight across at the ruler guide.

6 Continue dragging around the
lettuces

When you reach the starting point
of the marquee, release the mouse

To finish the selection.

7 Deselect the selection   Press Ctrl+D.

Update the image   Press Ctrl+S.

The Quick Selection tool

Explanation

You can select areas with clearly defined edges by using the Quick Selection tool. Using the Quick Selection tool, click or drag over an area to select it. As you drag and select more areas of the image, the Quick Selection tool detects similar areas within defined edges and adds them to the selection.

After you've made a selection, you can add other areas or subtract areas. To add to a selection, click the "Add to selection" button, shown in Exhibit 2-1, and click or drag over another area of the image. (Note that the "Add to selection" button is selected automatically after you create a new selection.) Areas you add need not be contiguous with the original selection, so you can add an area from another part of the image. To remove a portion of an area you've selected, click the "Subtract from selection" button and click or drag over the area you want to deselect.

You can also press Shift to temporarily select the "Add to selection" button and Alt to temporarily select the "Subtract from selection" button.

To increase or decrease the Quick Selection brush size, change the settings in the Brush picker. By doing so, you can select more or less of an area. To quickly adjust the diameter of the brush, with the Quick Selection tool selected, press [or].

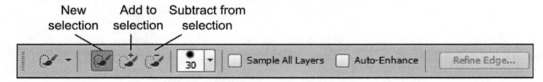

Exhibit 2-1: Options for the Quick Selection tool

Do it!

A-3:   **Selecting with the Quick Selection tool**

The files for this activity are in Student Data folder **Unit 2\Topic A**.

Here's how	Here's why
1 In the Tools panel, select [icon]	The Quick Selection tool.
On the options bar, click [icon]	(If necessary.) To specify that you'll create a new selection.
2 Drag slowly from top to bottom over the topmost head of lettuce	As you drag, the Quick Selection tool detects areas similar to the one you drag over. As you drag over more areas, the selection expands to include more of the lettuce.
Release the mouse and observe the options bar	[icons]
	After you release the mouse button, the "Add to selection" button is selected automatically.
3 Click and drag over the lettuce	To continue adding sections to the selection. Likely, Photoshop will include some areas you want to leave out.
4 Press (ALT) and click the indicated area	
	(At the right edge.) To remove it from the selection.
Remove the other unwanted areas of the selection	Press Alt and click or drag over the areas.
5 Update and close the image	

Topic B: Modifying selections

This topic covers the following ACE exam objectives for Photoshop CS6.

#	Objective
4.2	**Adding and subtracting from selections**
4.2.1	Adding and subtracting selections
4.2.2	Adding and subtracting of selections using different selection tools
4.2.3	Modifying selections

Refining a selection

Explanation

Regardless of which tool you use, it's often difficult to get a perfect selection the first time. Rather than starting over, you can modify a selection by adding to or subtracting from the selection marquee. You can even use different selection tools to add to or subtract from a selection. When you choose a selection tool (with the exception of the Quick Selection tool), the options bar displays four selection buttons that control the tool function, as shown in Exhibit 2-2.

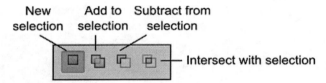

Exhibit 2-2: Selection options

The following table describes the selection options.

Button	Clicking or dragging with a selection tool...
New selection	Automatically deselects an existing selection and begins a new one. The New selection button is selected by default.
Add to selection	Selects parts of the image without deselecting the existing selection.
Subtract from selection	Deselects part of the existing selection.
Intersect with selection	Creates selections that intersect with existing selections, resulting in a selection made up only of the intersecting regions.

When the New selection button is selected on the options bar, you can refine a selection by temporarily activating the selection button you want.

- Press Shift to temporarily activate the "Add to selection" button.
- Press Alt to temporarily activate the "Subtract from selection" button.
- Press Shift+Alt to temporarily activate the "Intersect with selection" button.

Do it!

B-1:   Adding to and subtracting from a selection

The files for this activity are in Student Data folder **Unit 2\Topic B**.

Here's how	Here's why
1 Open Peaches 1	
Save the image in Photoshop format as **My peaches 1**	In the current topic folder.
2 Using the Rectangular Marquee tool, drag a marquee around the cardboard sign, as shown	
3 Select the Quick Selection tool	
On the options bar, click	(If necessary.) You'll add to the selection.
4 Drag to add the peaches to the selection	
5 Press ⟨ALT⟩ and drag around the cardboard sign	To remove unwanted areas from the selection.

6 Add and remove areas as desired	So that the selection contains mostly the sign and the peaches
7 Update and close the image	

Commands for modifying selections

Explanation Besides adding to or subtracting from a selection, you can use the commands in the Select menu's Modify submenu to change a selection. The following table describes the five commands in the Modify submenu.

Command	Description
Border	Selects only the pixels at the border of a selection, based on the width you specify.
Smooth	Makes a selection's edges more rounded, based on the value you specify.
Expand	Spreads a selection outward by the value you specify.
Contract	Shrinks a selection inward by the value you specify.
Feather	Blends a selection with its background by applying transparency to the selection's outer pixels.

Transforming a selection marquee

You can transform a selection marquee to more closely fit it to the area you want to select. For example, you can rotate or resize a selection marquee. To transform a selection:

1 Choose Select, Transform Selection. Handles appear around the selection.

2 Transform the selection so it fits to the area you want to select, as follows:

- Drag from within the selection to move the selection marquee.
- Drag the selection handles to scale the selection.
- Point outside the selection and drag to rotate the selection.

3 Press Enter to complete the transformation.

Transforming a selection doesn't affect the image; it changes only the shape, size, or angle of the selection marquee itself. If you want to cancel a change you're making, you can press Esc to return to the original selection.

Feathering

By default, Photoshop's selection tools all apply anti-aliasing to soften a selection's edges. However, anti-aliasing softens only the pixels at the very edge of the selection. If you want to soften a larger area, you can apply feathering. *Feathering* blends a selection with its background by applying transparency to the selection's outer pixels. As the feathering extends outward, it becomes increasingly transparent. The feathering isn't apparent until you move, cut, copy, or fill the selection.

You can specify feathering for the lasso tools and marquee tools by entering a value in the Feather box on the options bar. The Feather value you specify won't affect an existing selection but will apply to new selections you make. The feathering extends equally inside and outside the selection edge, as shown in Exhibit 2-3.

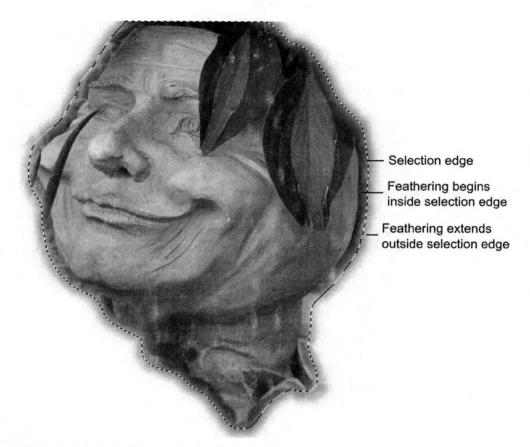

— Selection edge

Feathering begins
inside selection edge

Feathering extends
outside selection edge

Exhibit 2-3: A selection with a feathered edge

You can also apply feathering to a selection by choosing Select, Modify, Feather and entering a value in the Feather Radius box.

The Select Inverse command

Sometimes the quickest way to select part of an image is to select the part of the image you *don't* want, and then choose Select, Inverse to select only the part of the image that wasn't selected. For example, to select a multi-colored umbrella on a solid white background, you could use the Magic Wand tool to select the white background, and then choose Select, Inverse to select only the umbrella.

Filling selected areas

After you select part of an image, you can fill it with a color, such as the current foreground or background color. The bottom of the Tools panel shows the current foreground and background colors. If you want to add the current foreground or background color to a selection, you can use several techniques:

- Choose Edit, Fill to open the Fill dialog box. From the Use list, select Foreground Color or Background Color, and then click OK. You can also press Delete or Backspace to open the Fill dialog box.
- Press Ctrl+Delete or Ctrl+Backspace to fill a selection on any layer with the background color.
- Press Alt+Delete or Alt+Backspace to fill a selection with the foreground color.

The Move tool

You can move a selection marquee by using a selection tool to drag from within the marquee. If you want to move the selected pixels themselves, however, use the Move tool to drag from within the marquee.

When you move a selection of pixels on the Background layer, the current background color fills the area previously occupied by the pixels. (The current background color is the color shown on the Set background color icon in the Tools panel.)

When you move selected pixels, they become a *floating selection*. A floating selection doesn't replace any pixels below it until you deselect it. Therefore, you can continue moving a floating selection without affecting the pixels below it. When you deselect a floating selection, the selected pixels replace the pixels below it.

Do it!

B-2: Modifying a selection

The files for this activity are in Student Data folder **Unit 2\Topic B**.

Here's how	Here's why
1 Open Planter 1	
Save the image in Photoshop format as **My planter 1**	In the current topic folder.
2 Select the Quick Selection tool	You want to emphasize the planter and give the image a stylized look.
3 Select the planter, as shown	
	You'll invert the selection so that the circular area containing the baby is not selected.
Choose **Select, Inverse**	To select only the area outside the selection you created.
Press ⟨CTRL⟩ + ⟨← BACKSPACE⟩	To fill the selected area with the current background color (white). This isn't the effect you were hoping for.

4 Choose **Edit, Undo Fill**	To restore the image. The selection is still active.
Press (CTRL) + (SHIFT) + (I)	To select the inverse of the selection.
5 Choose **Select, Modify, Feather...**	To open the Feather Selection dialog box.
Edit the Feather Radius box to read **30**	
Click **OK**	To apply the change.
6 Press (CTRL) + (SHIFT) + (I)	To select the inverse of the selection.
Press (CTRL) + (← BACKSPACE)	To fill the area surrounding the planter with white, this time with a feathered edge. The feathered section is close to the planter, and you want the fade to appear farther from it.
7 Press (CTRL) + (Z)	(Or choose Edit, Undo Fill.) To restore the image again.
Press (CTRL) + (SHIFT) + (I)	
8 Choose **Select, Modify, Expand...**	To open the Expand Selection dialog box.
Edit the Expand By box to read **50**	
Click **OK**	To move the selection out 50 pixels from the original selection. Note that the selection is still feathered.
9 Press (CTRL) + (SHIFT) + (I)	
Press (CTRL) + (← BACKSPACE)	
10 Deselect the image selection	
Update and close the image	

Unit summary: Image selections

Topic A   In this topic, you used the **marquee** tools, the **Lasso** tool, and the **Quick Selection** tool to select image areas.

Topic B   In this topic, you **added to and subtracted from a selection**. You also learned how to modify a selection by applying **feathering**.

Independent practice activity

In this activity, you'll select image areas and modify the selection.

The files for this activity are in Student Data folder **Unit 2\Unit summary**.

1 Open Apples 2, and save it as **My apples 2**.

2 Using the Quick Selection tool, select the apples in the foreground.

3 If necessary, add the stickers on the apples to the selection.

4 Feather the selection by **20 px**.

5 Inverse the selection, and fill the selection with a black color. (*Hint:* The keyboard shortcut you use to do this depends on whether black is the foreground or background color.)

6 Press Ctrl+H to hide the selection.

7 Undo the fill, then press Ctrl+H to show the selection

8 Remove the chalkboard sign from the selection.

9 Feather the selection by **30 px**, then fill it with a white color.

10 Update and close the file.

Review questions

1 How can you select a tool that isn't currently visible in the Tools panel?

    A Click and hold on the tool group to display a menu, then select the desired tool.

    B Press Shift and the tool's keyboard shortcut (for example, Shift+M).

    C Press Alt and click the tool group to cycle through the tools.

    D All of the above.

2 How can you most efficiently create a perfectly square selection?

    A Press Alt and use the Rectangular Marquee tool to drag to create the square.

    B Press Shift and use the Rectangular Marquee tool to drag to create the square.

    C Press Alt and use the Polygonal Lasso tool to click to add each of the square's corners.

    D Press Shift and use the Polygonal Lasso tool to click to add each of the square's corners.

3 Which tool should you use to create a freehand selection?

    A Lasso

    B Polygonal Lasso

    C Magnetic Lasso

    D Rectangular Marquee

4 To subtract from a selection, which key should you press as you use a selection tool?

    A Ctrl

    B Alt

    C Shift

    D F1

5 Softening a selection by gradually reducing opacity to a specified number of pixels extending equally inside and outside a selection edge is called _____.

6 True or false? If you want to move the selected pixels, rather than the selection marquee, you should drag with the Move tool, not a selection tool.

Unit 3

Layers

Complete this unit, and you'll know how to:

A Create empty layers, create layers based on a selection, arrange layers, and move layers from one image to another.

B Transform layers by using commands.

C Use type layers to add and format text.

D Use opacity and layer styles to apply effects to layers.

Topic A: Creating layers

This topic covers the following ACE exam objectives for Photoshop CS6.

#	Objective
5.1	**Creating and organizing layers**
5.1.1	Creating different types of layers and dragging under/over for visibility
5.1.2	Hiding and showing layers
5.1.3	Using keyboard shortcuts for moving and creating layers
5.1.4	Dragging and dropping images between documents

Creating new layers from selections

Explanation

By default, each new Photoshop image includes a single layer of pixels, which the Layers panel identifies as the Background layer. When you deselect a floating selection on the Background layer (for example, you move a selection with the Move tool), the selected pixels replace any pixels that were below them, maintaining a single layer.

You can isolate selected image pixels from the rest of an image by putting them on their own layer. By doing so, you can keep pixels on individual layers from affecting the pixels on other layers. Also, additional layers you add can contain empty or transparent areas, through which you can see the pixels in layers below.

One way to create a layer is to convert a selection of pixels to a new layer. To do so:

1   Select the part of the image that you want to move to a new layer.

2   Move the pixels to a new layer by doing either of the following:

- Choose Layer, New, Layer via Copy to create a layer containing a copy of the selected pixels. The original pixels remain on the original layer.

- Choose Layer, New, Layer via Cut to create a layer containing the selected pixels, removing them from the original layer.

3   The new layer is named "Layer 1" if it's the first new layer, "Layer 2" if it's the second, and so on. To rename it, double-click the layer name in the Layers panel, type a new name, and press Enter. (If you double-click to the right of the layer name or on the layer thumbnail, you'll open the Layer Style dialog box.)

You can also use these keyboard shortcuts to create new layers via copying or cutting:

- Press Ctrl+J to create a new layer via copy. Alternatively, press Ctrl+Alt+J to open the New Layer dialog box first, in which you can enter a layer name and select other options before creating the layer.

- Press Ctrl+Shift+J to create a new layer via cut. Alternatively, press Ctrl+Alt+Shift+J to open the New Layer dialog box first.

Working with the selected layer

When an image contains multiple layers, you can work with each layer's contents individually. The Layers panel indicates which layer is selected by highlighting its name, as shown in Exhibit 3-1. To select a layer, click it in the Layers panel. When a layer is selected, the actions you perform will apply to that layer's contents.

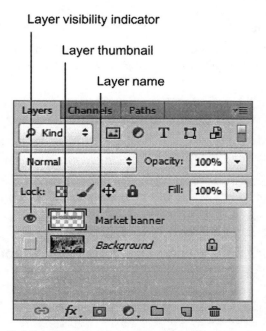

Exhibit 3-1: A selected layer in the Layers panel

Moving layer contents

After you move part of an image to a new layer, you can use the Move tool to move the layer contents within the image. However, if you want to move all of the pixels in a layer, you don't have to select them first; you can drag from any part of the layer, including empty areas, to move all pixels in that layer.

Hiding layer contents

If you want to hide the contents of a layer, click the eye icon to the left of the layer's name in the Layers panel. The eye icon will disappear, indicating that the layer is hidden. You can click the same spot to make the layer visible again.

Deleting layers

After you've added layers, you might need to delete them. Even if you don't end up using layers (for example, by hiding them), adding multiple layers to an image can greatly increase its file size.

To delete one or more layers, select the desired layers and do one of the following:

- In the Layers panel, click the Delete icon. A message box will appear, asking you to confirm the deletion.
- From the Layers panel menu, choose Delete Layer (or Delete Layers, if more than one layer is selected). A message box will appear, asking you to confirm the deletion.
- Drag the selected layers to the Delete icon in the Layers panel. Photoshop will delete the layers without displaying a confirmation message.
- Press the Delete key. Photoshop will delete the selected layers without displaying a confirmation message.

You might end up with one or more empty layers that you aren't using. To quickly delete all empty layers in an image, choose File, Scripts, Delete All Empty Layers.

Do it!

A-1: Creating a layer from a selection

The files for this activity are in Student Data folder **Unit 3\Topic A**.

Here's how	Here's why
1 Open Market with banner	
Save the image in Photoshop format as **My market with banner**	(In the current topic folder.) A colleague has sent you the draft of a project she's working on so that you can use the banner graphic. However, she sent a flattened image. You'll create a new layer from a selection.
2 Select the Rectangular Marquee tool	
Select the banner graphic, as shown	To isolate it from the background.

3 Press `CTRL` + `J`	To create a new layer by copying the selected pixels.
Click the **Layers** panel	(If necessary.) A new layer, named "Layer 1," has been created above the Background layer. The new layer is highlighted in the Layers panel, indicating that it's the active layer.

4 In the Layers panel, double-click **Layer 1**	(The layer name itself.) To select the layer name.
Type **Market banner** and press ⏎ ENTER	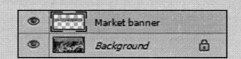
	To rename the layer.
5 On the Tools panel, click	To select the Move tool.
Point anywhere in the image and drag down	To move the contents of the active layer. Because you moved the text on this layer, you can now see the banner on the Background layer below it.
6 In the Layers panel, next to the Background layer, click 👁	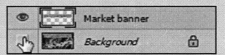
	To hide the Background layer. The eye icon disappears when you click it, indicating that the layer's contents are hidden.
Observe the transparent space around the image	The checkerboard pattern represents transparent space.
Drag anywhere in the transparent space	To observe that you can move the layer contents.
7 Update the image	

Moving layers between images

Explanation

Another way to create layers is to move a selection or layer from one image to another. When you move a layer to a new image, you can drag the layer from the image itself, or you can drag the layer name from the Layers panel. When you drag the layer to another image window, the layer contents appear in that image, and the layer appears in the Layers panel for that image. If, rather than moving a layer, you move a selection to a new image, the layer is named "Layer 1" in the image it moves to.

When you drag a layer to another image with the same pixel dimensions (width and height in pixels) as the original image, the layer contents will appear at the same relative position as in the original image. If the dimensions don't match, then pressing Shift as you drag the layer between windows centers the layer contents in the new image.

You can also drag a file from your Windows Explorer into Photoshop to create a layer. When you drag a file from a folder or the desktop into Photoshop, Photoshop creates a new layer in the current image and automatically centers and sizes it proportionally to fit in the image.

Copying selections between images

Another way to transfer content from one image to another is by copying and pasting. To do so, select the area you want to copy, and choose Edit, Copy or press Ctrl+C. Then switch to the image where you want to place the selection. Paste the content by using one of the following Paste commands:

- **Edit, Paste** (or Ctrl+V) — Pastes the copied content at the center of the image. However, if an area is selected, the copied content is pasted over the selection.

- **Edit, Paste Special, Paste in Place** (or Shift+Ctrl+V) — Pastes the copied content in the same relative position as its position in the image from where it was copied.

- **Edit, Paste Special, Paste Into** (or Alt+Shift+Ctrl+V) — If an area is selected, pastes the copied content into the center of the selection, maintaining the content's original size.

- **Edit, Paste Special, Paste Outside** — If an area is selected, pastes the copied content outside of the selection, maintaining the content's original size. Therefore, if the selection is larger than the copied content, the content will be hidden.

Each Paste command creates a new layer, containing the pasted content, in the image.

Using *n*-up views

When working with multiple images, you might want to arrange them so that you can see more than one at a time. To do so, choose Window, Arrange, and select an option from the submenu. The options available will depend on how many images are open.

Do it!   **A-2:   Moving a layer to another image**

The files for this activity are in Student Data folder **Unit 3\Topic A**.

Here's how	Here's why
1 Open Corn 2	
Save the image in Photoshop format as **My corn 2**	You'll move the Market banner layer from the "My market with banner" image into this image.
2 Choose **Window**, **Arrange**, **2-up Vertical**	To position the two image windows so that both can be seen.
Click the **My market with banner.psd 2** tab	
3 Press ⌈SHIFT⌉ and drag the **Market banner** layer from the Layers panel to the "My corn 2" window	To add the banner layer to the picture of the ears of corn, centering the layer vertically and horizontally in the image.
4 Update and close My market with banner	
Update My corn 2	

Creating empty layers

Explanation Another way to create a layer is to click the "Create a new layer" icon in the Layers panel. This creates a blank layer above the layer that's selected in the Layers panel. You can double-click the layer name to rename it. Alternatively, if you press Alt and click the "Create a new layer" icon, you'll open the New Layer dialog box, in which you can enter a layer name and select other options.

The keyboard shortcut for creating a new empty layer is Ctrl+Shift+N. Using the keyboard shortcut opens the New Layer dialog box first. If you press Ctrl+Alt+Shift+N, however, you create a new empty layer without opening the dialog box.

Filling layers and selections

You can fill layers with a color, such as the current foreground or background color; you can use the same technique to fill a selection. The bottom of the Tools panel shows the current foreground and background colors, as shown in Exhibit 3-2. If you want to use the current foreground or background color to fill a layer or a selection, you can use several techniques:

- Choose Edit, Fill to open the Fill dialog box. From the Use list, select Foreground Color or Background Color, and then click OK. You can also press Delete or Backspace to open the Fill dialog box.
- Press Ctrl+Delete or Ctrl+Backspace to fill a selection on any layer with the background color.
- Press Alt+Delete or Alt+Backspace to fill a selection with the foreground color.

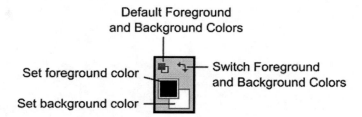

Exhibit 3-2: The color indicators and buttons in the Tools panel

Layer stacking order

When you create a layer, it appears above whichever layer is currently selected. The content of a layer overlaps the content of any layers that are below it in the Layers panel. If you want to change the layer stacking order, drag the layers up or down in the Layers panel. You can also choose an option from the Layer, Arrange submenu.

Do it!   **A-3:   Creating and filling empty layers**

Here's how	Here's why
1 In the Layers panel, select the **Market banner** layer	If necessary.
2 Select the Rectangular Marquee tool	You know you want to fill the bottom half of the image with something, but you're not yet sure what; you'll create a placeholder using an empty layer.
Select the bottom half of the image, as shown	
3 Press `CTRL` + `SHIFT` + `N`	To open the New Layer dialog box.
Edit the Name box to read **Bottom panel**	
Click **OK**	To create an empty layer. Because the new layer is automatically selected, the selection marquee is now active on the new layer.
4 Press `CTRL` + `← BACKSPACE`	To fill the current selection with the background color. The white fill is added to the layer.
5 In the Layers panel, drag the **Bottom panel** layer below the Market banner layer, as shown	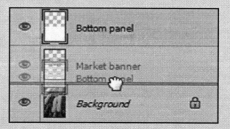
	To make the entire Market banner layer visible in the image.
6 Deselect the selection	
Update and close the image	

Topic B: Transform controls

This topic covers the following ACE exam objectives for Photoshop CS6.

#	Objective
7.3	**Using the transform controls**
7.3.1	Using the transform controls to scale, rotate, and copy images
7.3.2	Using keyboard modifier combinations for effective usage

The Free Transform command

Explanation

You can apply a number of transformations to individual layers or selections to modify them. The transform controls are located in the Edit menu and, when selected, apply transformations to the currently selected layer or any layer pixels currently selected.

The most versatile transform control is the Free Transform command. To use it:

1 Select the content you want to transform.

- In the Layers panel, select the layer containing the content you want to transform.
- Use a selection tool to select the area you want to transform.

2 Choose Edit, Free Transform or press Ctrl+T. Transform handles appear around the selected content, and the reference point appears in the center. The *reference point* determines the point around which any transformations occur.

3 If desired, drag the reference point within the transform borders. For example, moving the point to the bottom-left corner will allow you to rotate the item around its bottom-left corner.

4 Transform the item by doing any of the following:

- To move the item, drag from within the transform border.
- To scale the item, drag the transform handles. To scale the item proportionally, press Shift as you drag a corner handle.
- To rotate the item, drag from outside the transform border. Press Shift as you rotate to constrain the rotation to 15° increments.
- To skew the item, press Ctrl and drag a transform handle.
- To create a perspective effect, press Ctrl+Alt+Shift and drag a transform handle.

5 To apply the transformations, press Enter. Or, to remove the transform handles without accepting the changes, press Esc.

Values for the transformations you apply appear on the options bar. As you drag a layer or selection to transform it, you can note the percentage you're increasing or decreasing it, or you can enter specific values on the options bar.

Aligning and distributing layers

You can align layers with other layers, or you can align layers with a selection border. In addition, you can distribute three or more layers evenly in an image.

To align layers with one another: In the Layers panel, select the layers you want to align. Then choose Layer, Align, and choose a command from the submenu.

To align layers with a selection border: First make a selection in the image; then, in the Layers panel, select the layers you want to align with the selection. Choose Layer, Align Layers To Selection, and choose a command from the submenu.

To distribute three or more layers evenly in an image: First align them, and then use the Layer, Distribute submenu. For example, to arrange photos of employees along the left edge of a background, first select the layers with the employee photos, as well as the Background layer. After you've aligned the layers, select only the employee photos and choose an option from the Layer, Distribute submenu.

You can also use the Align and Distribute buttons on the options bar when layers are selected.

Do it!

B-1: Using the Free Transform command

The files for this activity are in Student Data folder **Unit 3\Topic B**.

Here's how	Here's why
1 Open Market flyer 1	
Save the image as **My market flyer 1**	(In the current topic folder.) You'll resize the Market banner layer so that it fits in the image. First, you decide you want to change the orientation of the image.
2 Choose **Image**, **Image Rotation, 90° CW**	
3 Verify that the Market banner layer is selected	
Press (CTRL) + (T)	(The keyboard shortcut for the Free Transform command.) Transform handles and a transform border appear around the layer.
4 Point just outside a corner of the selection	
	The pointer changes to indicate that you can rotate the selection.
Press (SHIFT) and drag to the left	To rotate the layer counterclockwise. Pressing Shift constrains the rotation to 15° increments.
Rotate the layer 90° counterclockwise	

5 Press ALT + SHIFT and drag the
   top-right handle up and to the
   right, as shown

	To resize the layer to fit the width of the image. Pressing Alt+Shift transforms the selection proportionally from the center.
Press ↵ ENTER	To commit the transformation.
6 Press CTRL and select the Background layer	To select both the Market banner and the Background layers. You'll align the tops of the layers.

   Choose **Layer**, **Align**,
   Top Edges

7 Select the **Bottom panel** layer

8 Press CTRL + T

   Press SHIFT + CTRL and drag
   the bottom-right handle as shown

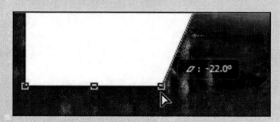

To skew the layer.

   Press ↵ ENTER

9 Update the image

Other transform options

Explanation

You can also perform a single transformation on a selection or layer by choosing a command from the Edit, Transform submenu:

- **Scale** — Scales the selected layer horizontally, vertically, or both around a reference point.
- **Rotate** — Rotates the selected layer around the reference point.
- **Skew** — Slants the selected layer vertically or horizontally.
- **Distort** — Stretches the selected layer in any direction.
- **Perspective** — Applies perspective to the selected layer.
- **Warp** — Warps the shape of the selected layer.

Transforming the Background layer

The only layer you can't move or transform is the Background layer. To turn it into a regular layer, double-click it to open the New Layer dialog box; then rename it (or leave the default name as Layer 0), and click OK. You can then move that layer in the stacking order and apply transformations to it.

Do it!

B-2: Using the Warp command

The files for this activity are in Student Data folder **Unit 3\Topic B**.

Here's how	Here's why
1 Double-click the **Background** layer	To open the New Layer dialog box. You'll apply a transformation to it. First, you need to convert it to a regular layer.
Edit the Name box to read **Corn**	
Click **OK**	
2 Choose **Edit**, **Transform**, **Warp**	
3 Drag the bottom-right handle up and to the left, as shown	Until the layer begins to overlap itself, creating a "page curl" effect.
Press ⏎ ENTER	
4 Update and close the image	

Topic C: Using type layers

This topic covers the following ACE exam objectives for Photoshop CS6.

#	Objective
8.1	**Using character and paragraph styles**
8.1.1	Creating and modifying character and paragraph styles
8.1.2	Best practices for creating reusable styles
8.1.3	Clearing style formats from a document
8.1.4	Font usage considerations
8.1.5	OpenType considerations

Creating type layers

Explanation

You can use Photoshop's Horizontal Type tool to add text to an image. When you begin adding text, a new type layer is automatically created to hold it. The text you add to the type layer is editable, so you can return to it at any time to edit or format it.

Because the text is editable, you can't work with it the same way you work with image areas made up of pixels. You can, however, convert editable text to pixels. You can then work with the text by using the same techniques you'd use to work with other image areas. But you can't edit or format the text after it's converted.

To add text to an image:

1   In the Tools panel, click the Horizontal Type tool.

2   In the image, click where you want to begin adding text. An insertion point will appear where you clicked, and a type layer will appear in the Layers panel.

3   On the options bar, shown in Exhibit 3-3, specify formatting options.

4   To specify the text color, click the "Set the text color" button on the options bar to open the Select text color dialog box. Click or enter values to select a color, and then click OK. You can also use the Color and Swatches panels.

5   Type to add the desired text to the image.

6   To change the formatting, select the text you want to format and then specify formatting options on the options bar. There are several ways to select text:

- Drag across the text to select it.
- Double-click to select one word.
- Triple-click to select all text on a single line.
- Click four times to select all text in a paragraph.
- Click five times, or choose Select, All, to select all text on the type layer.

7   On the options bar, click the "Commit any current edits" button to apply your changes and exit edit mode. Or cancel the current edits and exit edit mode by pressing Esc or by clicking the "Cancel any current edits" button.

You can move and transform type layers just as you'd move and transform pixel-based layers. Before you move or transform text, though, be sure to exit edit mode.

Exhibit 3-3: Formatting options when a Type tool is selected

Do it!

C-1: Adding text to an image

The files for this activity are in Student Data folder **Unit 3\Topic C**.

Here's how	Here's why
1 Open Market flyer 2	
Save the image as **My market flyer 2**	
2 Select the **Bottom panel** layer	You'll create a new type layer, and you want it to appear above this layer.
3 In the Tools panel, click [T.]	The Horizontal Type tool.
4 On the options bar, from the Font Family menu, choose **Arial**	
From the Font Style menu, choose **Black**	
Edit the Font Size box to read **72**	To set the type size to 72 points.
5 In the image, click at the top of the blank white area	To add the insertion point and create a type layer.
Type **This weekend**	
On the options bar, click [✓]	(The "Commit any current edits" button.) To exit edit mode and apply the changes.

6 Observe the Layers panel	The type layer is automatically named "This weekend," based on the text contained in the layer.
7 Double-click the This weekend layer icon	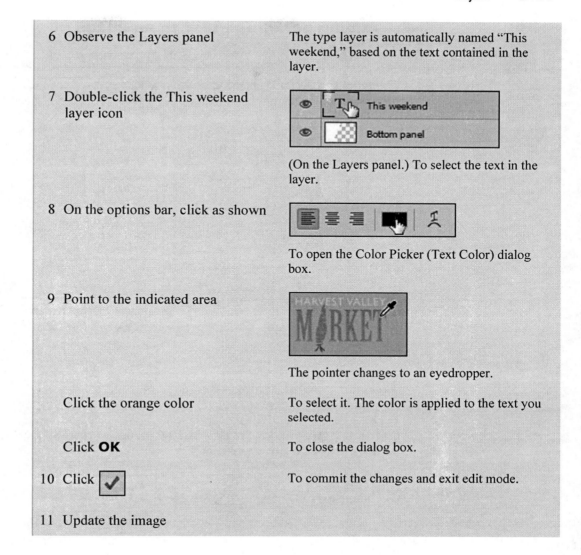
	(On the Layers panel.) To select the text in the layer.
8 On the options bar, click as shown	
	To open the Color Picker (Text Color) dialog box.
9 Point to the indicated area	
	The pointer changes to an eyedropper.
Click the orange color	To select it. The color is applied to the text you selected.
Click **OK**	To close the dialog box.
10 Click	To commit the changes and exit edit mode.
11 Update the image	

Paragraph text

Explanation   When you add text with a Type tool, the text won't wrap to a new line until you press Enter. The text you add when you click on an image with a Type tool is called *point text*. If you want to create text that automatically wraps within a designated border, you can use a Type tool to specify a *bounding box* by dragging in the image. Text you add within a bounding box is called *paragraph text*.

Do it!

C-2: Adding paragraph text to an image

Here's how	Here's why
1 Using the Horizontal Type tool, drag to create a rectangular bounding box, as shown	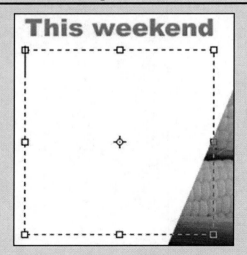

To create a type layer with a defined area for paragraph text.

2 On the options bar, set the text formatting to **Arial**, **Italic**, **48 pt**

3 Type
Come try the latest from your favorite vendors, and sample what's new at the market!

Drag to adjust the width of the text boundary so the text re-flows as shown

If necessary.

4 Click ✔

5 Update the image

Text formatting

To format or edit text on a type layer, you must be in edit mode. To switch to edit mode to edit or format existing text:

- Use a Type tool to click existing text on a type layer.
- Using any tool, double-click the thumbnail next to a type layer in the Layers panel to automatically switch to the Type tool and select all text on that layer.

Although you can specify some text formatting by using the options bar, you can select from a greater number of options by using the Character panel, shown in Exhibit 3-4, and the Paragraph panel, shown in Exhibit 3-5. You can open these panels by clicking the "Toggle the Character and Paragraph panels" button on the options bar when a type tool is selected or by choosing Window, Character or Window, Paragraph.

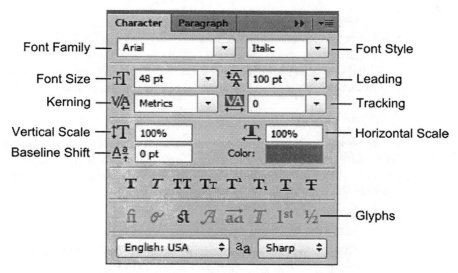

Exhibit 3-4: The Character panel

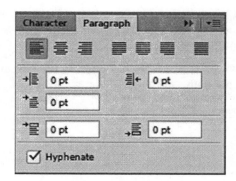

Exhibit 3-5: The Paragraph panel

The following table explains some of the settings available in the Character panel.

Setting	Description
Kerning	Increases or decreases the horizontal space between specific pairs of characters, as opposed to several characters or whole blocks of text.
Leading	Adjusts the vertical space between lines of type.
Tracking	Loosens or tightens spacing between selected characters or blocks of text, rather than between specific pairs of characters, as with kerning.

Character and paragraph styles

A new feature in Photoshop CS6 is the addition of character and paragraph styles. You can use styles to format characters or paragraphs quickly and consistently. A *style* is a set of formatting specifications saved under one name. For example, you can create a style that contains specifications such as 24-pt Arial, bold, and justified alignment. After you create this style, you can apply it to any text in an image.

Paragraph styles

A *paragraph style* is applied to entire paragraphs. It can contain both paragraph formatting and character formatting. You can create a style based on existing formatting, or you can create a style by entering values for formatting options. To create a paragraph style based on existing formatting:

1 Format text as desired.

2 Place the insertion point in the formatted text.

3 Choose Window, Paragraph to open the Paragraph panel.

4 Click the "Create new Paragraph Style" button at the bottom of the panel. A new style named Paragraph Style, followed by a number, appears in the list. This style contains the formatting of the selected text.

5 Double-click the style name to open the Paragraph Style Options dialog box, shown in Exhibit 3-6, so you can edit the style's properties or change its name. When you're done changing settings, click OK.

To apply a style to a paragraph, place the insertion point in the paragraph. Then, in the Paragraph Styles panel, click the name of the style you want to apply.

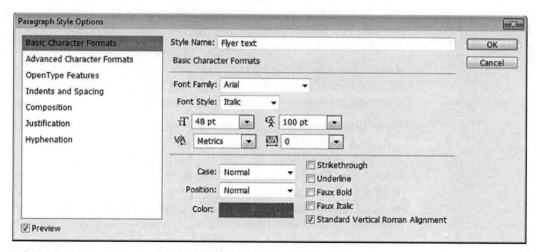

Exhibit 3-6: The Paragraph Style Options dialog box

Character styles

A *character style* is similar to a paragraph style, with two major differences. First, a character style can contain only character formatting. Second, character styles can be applied to individual characters, whereas paragraph styles uniformly format all text on a particular layer.

As with paragraph styles, it's easiest to define a character style by selecting text that already contains the formatting that you want for the style.

To create a character style:

1 Select the formatted text that you want to use to create a character style.
2 In the Character Styles panel, click the "Create new Character Style" button.
3 Double-click the style name to open the Character Style Options dialog box. When you're done changing settings, click OK.

Overriding local formatting

When text has a paragraph style applied to it, it is formatted with the attributes defined in the style. But the text can also have additional formatting (for example, if you've italicized a single word in the paragraph). The additional formatting is referred to as a *local override* or *local formatting* and will always take precedence over the style. When you select text that includes local formatting, a plus sign appears next to the style's name in the Paragraph Styles panel. To remove any local formatting in a paragraph, click the Clear Override button in the Paragraph Styles or the Character Styles panel.

Font usage considerations

There are a few things to consider when using text in an image. First, if you're using a file that contains a text layer that uses an uncommon font, you might run into trouble when opening that file on a different computer—for example, when sending the file to a colleague. If the font used in the image isn't available and you try to edit the text layer, you'll see a warning message indicating the font is missing and that it will be replaced before you can edit the text. Accepting the font substitution will replace the font originally used.

One way to avoid issues with missing fonts is to rasterize text layers. This converts the layer from a vector layer to a raster layer—essentially, rasterizing converts the editable text into a picture of the text. You can still transform and edit the pixels on a rasterized layer, but you won't be able to use the type tools to edit the text.

Another consideration is the usage of OpenType fonts. OpenType uses a single file for both Windows and Macintosh operating systems, avoiding some problems with font substitution and text flowing differently introduced by fonts that use separate files for different operating systems.

Some OpenType fonts also contain alternate forms for specific characters. These forms of a character are called *glyphs* and include such things as ligatures, ornaments, and fractions. Not all fonts contain glyphs, and not all fonts that contain glyphs contain the same ones. By default, if a font contains them, then glyps are enabled in Photoshop, with the exception of discretionary glyphs, which are stylistic replacements for certain pairs of letters. To enable or disable glyphs, display the panel menu and choose an option from the OpenType submenu. You also can use the glyph buttons on the Character panel, shown in Exhibit 3-4.

Do it!

C-3: Creating paragraph styles

Here's how	Here's why
1 Double-click the Come try the latest… layer icon	To select all of the text on the layer.
2 On the options bar, click 🖽	To display the Character panel. You'll adjust the leading.
Point to the leading icon, as shown	You'll scrub the leading value to change the vertical space between the lines of text.
Drag to the right to scrub the leading value	Dragging to the right increases the tracking value.
When the tracking value is **100 pt**, release the mouse button	

3 Choose **Window**, **Paragraph Styles**	To open the Paragraph Styles panel. You'll save these settings so you can reuse them.
In the Paragraph Styles panel, click 	(The Create new Paragraph Style button.) To add a new paragraph style, Paragraph Style 1, that uses the formatting of the selected text.
4 Double-click **Paragraph Style 1**	To open the Paragraph Style Options dialog box.
Edit the Style Name box to read **Flyer text**	
5 Click the Color box	To open the Color Picker (Text Color) dialog box.
Using the eyedropper, select a dark green color	

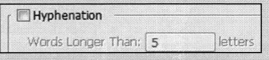

Click **OK**	
6 At the left of the Paragraph Style Options dialog box, click **Hyphenation**	
Clear **Hyphenation**	

Hyphenation
Words Longer Than: 5   letters

To prevent text using this style from hyphenating.

Click **OK**	
7 Hide the Paragraph Styles panel	Click the double-arrow button in the panel's top-right corner.
8 Update and close the image	

Topic D: Using layer effects

This topic covers the following ACE exam objectives for Photoshop CS6.

#	Objective
8.5	**Working with layer styles**
8.5.1	Accessing layer styles from multiple areas in Photoshop
8.5.2	Adding several styles threaded together to create a specific style

Layer styles and opacity

Explanation

When an image includes layers, you can apply effects to individual layers to change their appearance and to adjust how each layer interacts with the others. For example, you can lower a layer's opacity so you can see through it to the layer below. You can also apply layer styles.

Layer opacity

A simple way to change a layer's opacity is to specify a value in the Opacity box in the Layers panel. At 100% opacity, a layer is solid, and you can't see through it at all. At 0% opacity, the layer is completely invisible (transparent). Lowering a layer's opacity is useful whenever you want underlying layers to be partially visible.

There are several ways to change the selected layer's opacity:

- Edit the value in the Opacity box.
- Click the triangle to the right of the Opacity box, and drag the Opacity slider that appears.
- With the Move tool selected, type a single number to specify opacity in increments of 10%. For example, typing 1 specifies 10% opacity, 2 specifies 20%, and so on. Typing 0 (zero) specifies 100% opacity. Type two digits quickly to specify that opacity value.

Do it!

D-1: Adjusting opacity

The files for this activity are in Student Data folder **Unit 3\Topic D**.

Here's how	Here's why
1 Open Market flyer 3	
Save the image as **My market flyer 3**	In the current topic folder.
2 Select the **Bottom panel** layer	You'll reduce the opacity of the layer so that the pixels underneath will show through partially.
3 In the Layers panel, scrub Opacity	To experiment with different opacity values.
Set the Opacity level to **70%**	
4 Update the image	

Layer styles

Explanation

Another way to apply an effect to a layer is to apply a layer style. *Layer styles* apply effects such as drop shadows and inner glows to an entire layer. Like blending modes, layer styles are nondestructive, so you can modify or remove them at any time.

You can apply a layer style by using the Layer Style dialog box. To open the Layer Style dialog box, do any of the following:

- In the Layers panel, click the "Add a layer style" icon and select the layer style you want to apply.

- Choose Layer, Layer Style. From the submenu that appears, choose the layer style you want to apply.

- In the Layers panel, double-click a pixel-based layer's thumbnail, or double-click to the right of the layer name for non-pixel-based or type layers.

To apply a style without displaying its options, check the style's checkbox in the Styles list in the Layer Style dialog box. To apply a style and display its options, you must click the style's name in the list (doing this will also check the style's checkbox). After specifying all of the style settings you want to use, click OK.

Do it!

D-2: Applying layer styles

Here's how	Here's why
1 In the Layers panel, double-click the space to the right of the This weekend layer's name, as shown	To open the Layer Style dialog box.
Move the dialog box	(If necessary.) So that you can see the text in the image. By default, Preview is checked in the dialog box, so you can observe the effect of changes you make while keeping the dialog box open.
2 On the left side of the dialog box, in the Styles list, click the words **Drop Shadow**	To select the Drop Shadow layer style and display its settings.
3 Set the Angle value to **145**	(Use the dial or enter the value.) To change the shadow's angle.
Set the Distance value to **10**	
Set the Size value to **20**	

4 In the Styles list, select **Stroke**

(Click the word "Stroke," not its checkbox.) To apply the Stroke style and display the Stroke settings for the type layer. You'll use the default settings.

5 At the top of the Styles list, select **Blending Options: Default**

From the Blend Mode list, select **Color Burn**

6 Click **OK**

To close the Layer Style dialog box and apply the settings to the image.

Next, you'll hide and then show the layer effects to see how the settings you created for the layer affect the image.

7 In the Layers panel, observe the This weekend layer

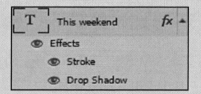

Note the effects applied to the layer.

To the left of "Stroke", click 👁

To hide the Stroke effect.

Turn the Stroke effect back on

Click the area to the left of the effect name.

Hide and show the Drop Shadow effect

8 Update and close the image

Unit summary: Layers

Topic A   In this topic, you created a **layer** based on pixels copied from an existing layer. Then you **moved a layer** from one image to another. You also created an empty layer and added a **fill** to part of that layer, and you adjusted the **layer stacking order**.

Topic B   In this topic, you learned how to use the **Free Transform** command and the **Warp** commands to transform layers.

Topic C   In this topic, you used the Horizontal Type tool to create **type layers** containing point text and paragraph text. You also learned how to format text on type layers. In addition, you created **paragraph styles**.

Topic D   In this topic, you adjusted **layer opacity** by using the Opacity box in the Layers panel. You also used the Layer Style dialog box to apply **layer styles**.

Independent practice activity

In this activity, you'll move layers between images and arrange layers. You'll also transform layer content, and you'll add and format text.

The files for this activity are in Student Data folder **Unit 3\Unit summary**.

1 Open Practice flyer and save the image as **My practice flyer**.

2 Open Apples 3. Then arrange the windows so that you can see both images at the same time.

3 Drag the Background layer from Apples 3 into My practice flyer and rename the layer **Apples**. Close Apples 3 without saving.

4 Drag the apples layer below the Corn layer.

5 Transform the apples layer so that the stickers on the apples aren't showing, as shown in Exhibit 3-7. (*Hint*: Use the Free Transform tool.)

6 Apply the Drop Shadow layer style to the Corn layer, using settings similar to those shown in Exhibit 3-8.

7 Add a new type layer with the text **See what's in store!**

8 Format the text as Arial, Bold Italic, 145-pt with 120-pt leading. Right-align the text and give it a white color. Position the type layer as shown in Exhibit 3-9. (*Hint:* Press Enter in the text to make it wrap to a new line. Remember to commit the changes when you're done.)

9 Position the type layer you added below the Corn layer, so that the type appears to be on the layer with the apples.

10 Update and close the image.

Exhibit 3-7: The My practice flyer image as it appears after Step 5

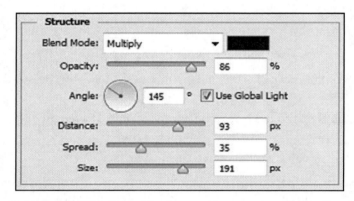

Exhibit 3-8: The Drop Shadow settings to specify for Step 6

Exhibit 3-9: The My practice flyer image as it appears after Step 8

Review questions

1 How can you add a layer that contains a copy of the current selection's pixels?

   A Click the "Create a new layer" icon in the Layers panel.

   B Press Alt and click the "Create a new layer" icon in the Layers panel.

   C Press Ctrl and click the "Create a new layer" icon in the Layers panel.

   D Choose Layer, New, Layer via Copy.

2 How can you arrange a layer so that its contents overlap the contents of all other layers? [Choose all that apply.]

   A Drag the layer to the top of the Layers panel.

   B Drag the layer to the bottom of the Layers panel.

   C Choose Layer, Arrange, Bring to Front.

   D Choose Layer, Arrange, Send to Back.

3 How can you select multiple layers in the Layers panel?

   A Click the top layer you want to select, and from the Layers panel menu, choose Merge Down.

   B Press Alt and click each layer you want to select in the Layers panel.

   C Right-click each layer you want to select in the Layers panel.

   D Press Ctrl and click each layer you want to select in the Layers panel.

4 What is the keyboard shortcut for the Free Transform command?

   A Ctrl+F.

   B Ctrl+T.

   C Alt+F.

   D Alt+T.

5 To make multiple lines of text wrap automatically within a rectangular border, you need to create:

   A Paragraph text.

   B Point text.

   C Wrap text.

   D You can't wrap multiple lines of text automatically in Photoshop.

6 True or false? If you want to reuse text formatting and apply it only to specific characters, use a paragraph style.

7 True or false? Double-clicking a type layer's "T" thumbnail switches to the Horizontal Type tool and selects all of the text on that layer.

8 To make a layer's pixels appear semi-transparent, lower its _____.

9 How can you open the Layer Style dialog box to add a layer style? [Choose all that apply.]

A Press Alt and click the "Create a new layer" icon in the Layers panel.

B Choose Layer, Layer Style, and from the submenu that appears, choose the layer style you want to apply.

C In the Layers panel, click the "Add a layer style" icon and select the layer style you want to apply.

D In the Layers panel, select a style from the Blending mode list.

10 Which of the following statements about layer styles are true? [Choose all that apply.]

A They are applied irreversibly to the layer's pixels.

B A layer style applied to a single layer can include both a drop shadow and a glow.

C You control their settings in the Layer Style dialog box.

D You can apply them to image layers, but not to type layers.

Unit 4

Basic image adjustments

Complete this unit, and you'll know how to:

A Use automatic adjustments to maximize image contrast, locate image shadows and highlights, and set target points in a Levels adjustment layer.

B Use a Curves adjustment layer to adjust image contrast.

Topic A: Levels adjustments

This topic covers the following ACE exam objectives for Photoshop CS6.

#	Objective
6.1	**Differentiating between adjustment types**
6.1.1	Identifying the strengths and weaknesses of specific adjustments
6.1.2	Applying adjustment layers for dramatic effect or color correction
6.1.3	Blending adjustment types

Adjustment layers

Explanation

You can apply adjustments to an image in Photoshop by using the Image, Adjustments submenu. When you choose a command—such as Hue/Saturation—from this submenu, it opens a corresponding dialog box, in which you can change settings. When you change an image in this way, however, the edits you make are *destructive;* that is, they change the image pixels.

To make the same kinds of adjustments—Hue/Saturation, Levels, Brightness/Contrast, and so on—but without changing the image pixels, you can use an *adjustment layer* . You can then easily remove or hide that layer to return the image to its original appearance. In addition, you can continually modify an adjustment layer's settings to experiment with different values.

The Adjustments panel

You can use the Adjustments panel, shown in Exhibit 4-1, to create adjustment layers and to access many of the commands that are also found in the Image, Adjustments menu. Additionally, the Adjustments panel includes a series of presets you can use to simplify commonly used adjustments.

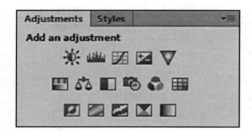

Exhibit 4-1: The Adjustments panel

Clicking each button creates a new adjustment layer. The following table describes the functions of each adjustment layer.

Button	Icon	Description
Brightness/ Contrast		Adjusts brightness and contrast values.
Levels		Sets pixel distribution for individual color channels.
Curves		Controls highlight, midtone, and shadow adjustments for individual channels.
Exposure		Adjusts tonality (primarily for HDR images).
Vibrance		Adjusts color saturation and minimizes clipping.
Hue/Saturation		Adjust hue, saturation, and lightness values.
Color Balance		Adjusts the overall mixture of colors in an image.
Black & White		Controls how an image is converted to high-contrast black and white.
Photo Filter		Simulates the effects of various photo filters.
Channel Mixer		Modifies a color channel.
Color Lookup		Remaps colors in the image to selected ones.
Invert		Creates a negative of the image.
Posterize		Specifies the number of tonal levels or brightness values per channel.
Threshold		Converts the image to high-contrast black and white. Pixels lighter than the specified threshold are converted to white, and pixels darker than the threshold are converted to black.
Selective Color		Adjusts the amount of process colors used in individual color components.
Gradient Map		Maps an image's grayscale range to the colors of a specified gradient fill.

Automatic adjustments

One way to apply adjustments is to use Photoshop's automatic adjustment options. You can apply automatic adjustments by choosing Image and then choosing Auto Tone, Auto Contrast, or Auto Color, but these commands result in destructive edits. A better method is to use the Adjustments panel, which provides automatic adjustment options that are layer-based and can be fine-tuned.

The Adjustments panel's Brightness/Contrast, Levels, and Curves options provide an Auto button that can make automatic tone and color corrections. You can use the Auto Color Correction Options dialog box, shown in Exhibit 4-2, to specify the type of automatic adjustment you want the Auto button to perform.

You also can select an option from the Preset list.

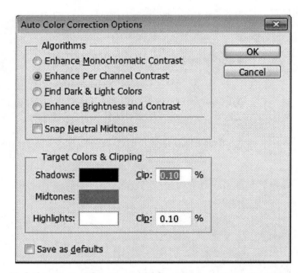

Exhibit 4-2: The Auto Color Correction Options dialog box

To specify the types of automatic adjustments that the Auto buttons make, follow these steps:

1   Create or select either a Levels or a Curves adjustment layer.

2   Open the Auto Color Correction Options dialog box by doing either of the following:

   • From the Adjustments panel menu, choose Auto Options.

   • In the Adjustments panel, press Alt and click the Auto button.

3   Select the correction algorithm you want to use:

   • **Enhance Monochromatic Contrast** — Makes shadows darker and light areas brighter, as you might by moving the input sliders to where the shadows and highlights begin on the Levels graph.

   • **Enhance Per Channel Contrast** — Adjusts each channel separately, as you might by moving the input sliders for individual channels to where each channel appears on the Levels graph.

   • **Find Dark & Light Colors** — Uses the lightest and darkest pixels as the shadow and highlight values.

   • **Enhance Brightness and Contrast** — Automatically applies monochromatic enhancement to the image.

4   Select Snap Neutral Midtones if you want Photoshop to choose a neutral color in your image and force it to gray.

5   Under Target Colors & Clipping, enter a Clip percentage for Shadows and Highlights to specify the percentage of extremes that will be eliminated from calculations. The default settings eliminate 0.10% of the darkest shadows and the brightest highlights from color-correction calculations.

6   By default, Photoshop uses neutral target colors: black for Shadows, gray for Midtones, and white for Highlights. To change a target color, click the color swatch and select a new target color.

7   Check "Save as defaults" to make your selections the default settings for the Auto buttons in the Adjustments panel and the Auto commands on the Image menu.

Undoing previous steps

As you work in Photoshop, you might need to undo one or more of your steps. If you need to return an image to a previous state, you can choose Edit, Undo. However, this command undoes only the most recent action. To undo multiple steps, you can use the History panel.

The History panel

The History panel tracks the actions you've performed after opening a file, and you can use it to undo any of the actions it lists. The most recent actions are at the bottom of the History panel, as shown in Exhibit 4-2.

To undo the steps listed in the History panel, you can use several techniques:

- Choose Edit, Step Backward or press Alt+Ctrl+Z to undo one step at a time.

- Choose Edit, Step Forward or press Shift+Ctrl+Z to redo one step at a time.

- In the History panel, click the action representing the image state to which you want to return. All actions more recent than the one you select are undone.

- Choose File, Revert to undo all actions you've performed since the last time you saved the image.

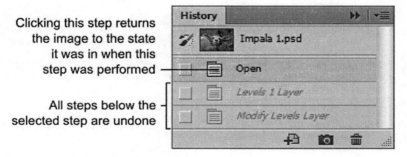

Clicking this step returns the image to the state it was in when this step was performed

All steps below the selected step are undone

Exhibit 4-3: The History panel

Do it!   ### A-1: Applying an automatic Levels adjustment

The files for this activity are in Student Data folder **Unit 4\Topic A**.

Here's how	Here's why
1 Open Impala 1	
Save the image as **My impala 1**	(In the current topic folder.) This image appears slightly washed out.
2 In the Adjustments panel, click ▦	(The Levels button.) To add a Levels adjustment layer to the image and to open the Properties panel.
3 Click **Auto**	Photoshop adjusts the image, but this isn't the effect you wanted.
Press ⌨CTRL⌨ + ⌨Z⌨	To undo the adjustment.
4 From the Properties panel menu, choose **Auto Options...**	To open the Auto Color Correction Options dialog box. The Enhance Brightness and Contrast option is selected by default.
5 Select **Enhance Monochromatic Contrast**	This option, which is equivalent to Auto Contrast, leaves a green cast in this image.
Select **Enhance Per Channel Contrast**	
6 Click **OK**	To close the dialog box. You'll undo the changes and modify the levels manually.
7 In the panel dock, click ▤	To display the History panel.
Scroll to the top of the History panel and click **Open**	
	To return to the original image as it appeared when you opened it.
Collapse the History panel	
8 Update the image	

The histogram

You can use the histogram in the Levels adjustment properties to quickly find an image's darkest and brightest pixels, which is useful for fine-tuning a Levels adjustment.

The *histogram*, shown in Exhibit 4-4, is the black area shown in the Properties panel when a Levels adjustment layer is selected. The histogram displays the number of pixels at each brightness level as a vertical line. The more pixels at a given brightness level, the taller the line. Because most images have a continuous range of tones, the lines often blend together to form a "mountainous" appearance.

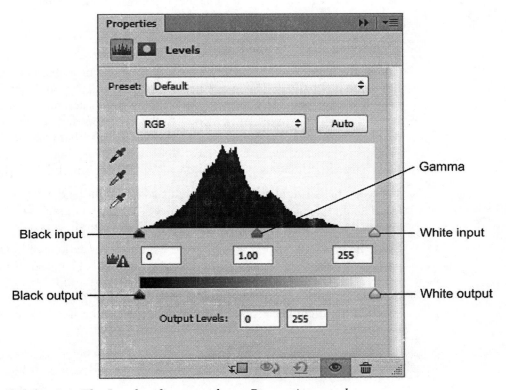

Exhibit 4-4: The Levels adjustment layer Properties panel

To fine-tune an image's contrast by adjusting its brightest areas (*highlights*), darkest areas (*shadows*), and *midtones*, drag the input sliders on the histogram:

- Drag the black input slider to the right to convert pixels that were originally dark colors to pure black.
- Drag the gamma slider to the left to brighten the midtones, or to the right to darken the midtones.
- Drag the white input slider to the left to convert pixels that were originally light colors to pure white.

Dragging either the black or the white input slider increases image contrast by moving more pixel colors toward the extremes (dark or light).

If an image's histogram does not extend all the way to the left or right, the image does not contain a full range of tones and usually has weak contrast. One approach to color-correcting such an image is to move the black and white input sliders until they reach the edges of the histogram; this forces the image's darkest pixels to black and its lightest pixels to white. Although this method of maximizing contrast often yields good results, it's not a failsafe formula because not all images should display the full range of tones from black to white.

Also, you can select a channel from the Channel list and adjust its levels separately to affect the image's color balance. For example, by choosing Red from the Channel list and dragging its gamma slider to the left, you make the image appear brighter red overall. The value 0 in a color channel represents none of that color, while 255 represents that color component fully saturated.

Identifying shadows and highlights

To use the histogram to find an image's darkest and brightest points, press Alt and drag the white input slider. The image becomes black, and as you drag to the left, the brightest areas begin to appear. If the brightest pixels are neutral, they'll appear white; but if the brightest pixels have a color tint, they'll appear as that color. If the brightest pixels have a color, the image might have a color cast that you should remove. If the brightest pixels are *supposed* to have a color, however, then the image probably doesn't have a true highlight and you shouldn't force the highlight to become neutral.

For example, a bright area on a colored surface might be the brightest area in an image, but it should display the color of the object's surface, not pure white. In this case, you should not set that area as the target highlight or neutralize its color.

Some images have *specular highlights*, which are reflections of light from a shiny surface. You should usually allow specular highlights to appear as pure white (R255 G255 B255), whereas other highlights should be closer to R245 G245 B245 (a bit darker than pure white). Also, you should avoid neutralizing an image based on a specular highlight because it might be pure white even if a color cast exists in the true highlights.

To use the histogram to find image shadows, press Alt and drag the black input slider. The image becomes pure white. As you drag, the darkest pixels begin to appear.

Color samplers

When you locate an image's target shadow and highlight, you can mark them with color samplers. You can then view the color values for those areas in the Info panel and see how your adjustments affect those values.

To add a color sampler, using the Eyedropper tool, press Shift and click in the image. A color sampler appears in the image as a small numbered icon, with a corresponding color value showing in the Info panel. You can press Shift and drag a color sampler to move it in an image. In addition, you can choose Color Samplers from the Info panel menu to hide or show the color samplers. To remove a color sampler, select the Eyedropper tool; then press Alt+Shift and click the color sampler.

Do it!

A-2: Locating shadows and highlights

Here's how	Here's why
1 In the Adjustments panel, click	You want to locate the shadow and highlight pixels before making a correction.
2 In the Properties panel, observe the histogram	It doesn't extend all the way to the left or right. This indicates that the image's shadows aren't as dark and its highlights aren't as bright as they could be.
3 Press (ALT) and drag the black input slider slowly to the right, until solid black appears	

To locate the shadows in the image.

The first areas that appear with color other than white are the darkest areas in the image. The largest area of solid black appears on the impala's horn, so you'll place the shadow color sampler there.

4 Select the Eyedropper tool Press (SHIFT) and click in the area you just identified	

To add a color sampler. The Info panel expands to display color values for point #1.

5 In the panel dock, click	To expand the Properties panel.
Press (ALT) and drag the white input slider to the left	

To locate the highlights. The first non-black area is the brightest in the image.

When the first non-black area appears, release (ALT)	To view the original image.
6 Press (SHIFT) and click to place a color sampler in a light area	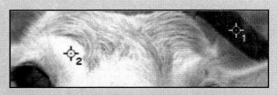

You'll also place color samplers for light and dark areas that should be neutral gray.

7 Update the image

Setting target points

You can use the Levels properties to specify the parts of the image that should be the highlights and the shadows. The area you specify as the *target highlight* will become the brightest part of the image, and the area you specify as the *target shadow* will become the darkest part of the image. Other image areas might match the brightness of the highlight or shadow target points, but no areas will be brighter than the highlight target or darker than the shadow target.

To set the target highlight and shadow:

1 Select a Levels adjustment layer and display the Properties panel.
2 Select the Set White Point tool, shown in Exhibit 4-5.
3 Point to the brightest part of the image and click. The point you clicked becomes the image highlight, and other image areas are adjusted accordingly.
4 Select the Set Black Point tool.
5 Point to the darkest part of the image and click. The point you clicked becomes the image shadow, and other image areas are adjusted accordingly.
6 Select the Set Gray Point tool.
7 Point to a midtone area of the image that should be neutral, and click. The point you clicked becomes neutral (with equal red, green, and blue values), and other image areas are adjusted accordingly.

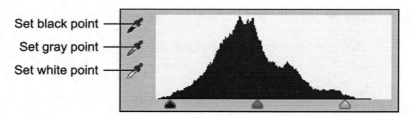

Exhibit 4-5: The target point tools for adjusting levels

Target values

By default, the image area that you specify as the target highlight is converted to pure white (255R 255G 255B), and the target shadow is converted to pure black (0R 0G 0B). However, it's a good idea to change the target highlight's brightness value to about 96% and to change the target shadow's brightness value to about 4%. Doing this is particularly useful for the following scenarios:

- If the area you target as the highlight is not the brightest part of the image, then it will be brightened to pure white (255R 255G 255B) by default; other areas that were brighter will also brightened to pure white. By converting several bright shades to pure white, you blow out the highlights, losing image detail. Similarly, setting the target shadow to pure black can block the shadows.

- Most printers can't reproduce detail in areas that are nearly pure white or nearly pure black. In addition, any area defined as pure white might not get any ink coverage on the paper, and this might look like a printing error.

Do it!

A-3: Setting target points with eyedroppers

Here's how	Here's why
1 Expand the Properties panel	Click its icon in the panel dock.
2 In the Properties panel, double-click	(The Set White Point tool.) To open the Color Picker (Target Highlight Color) dialog box. You'll select the white target color.
3 Edit the first B box to read **96**, as shown	

● H:	0	°	○ L:	97
○ S:	0	%	○ a:	0
○ B:	96	%	○ b:	0
○ R:	245		C:	3 %
○ G:	245		M:	2 %
○ B:	245		Y:	2 %
#	f5f5f5		K:	0 %

Here's how	Here's why
	(Use the B box beneath H and S, not the one beneath R and G.) The B value in the HSB color model stands for Brightness.
Click **OK**	To close the dialog box. Another dialog box appears, providing the option of saving the setting as a default value.
Click **No**	
4 Double-click	(The Set Black Point tool.) You'll set the black target color.
Edit the first B box to read **4**	Beneath H and S.
Click **OK**, then click **No**	To close the dialog box.
5 With the Set Black Point tool selected, click color sampler 1 in the image	To set that point to a neutral shadow with 4% brightness.
6 Select the Set White Point tool	
In the image, click color sampler 2	To set that point to a neutral highlight with 96% brightness.
7 In the Properties panel, click	To view the image's previous state.
8 Update and close the image	

Topic B: Curves adjustments

This topic covers the following ACE exam objectives for Photoshop CS6.

#	Objective
6.1	**Differentiating between adjustment types**
6.1.1	Identifying the strengths and weaknesses of specific adjustments
6.1.2	Applying adjustment layers for dramatic effect or color correction
6.2	**Using TAT, clipping, and visibility**
6.2.1	Working with the TAT

Using curves to adjust contrast

Explanation

You can use Levels adjustments to adjust image shadows, highlights, and midtones, but you can often adjust an image with greater precision by using Curves adjustments. For the most flexibility, you'll want to make your changes on a Curves adjustment layer so they are nondestructive.

The advantage of using the Curves adjustment is that you can adjust any specific brightness level, instead of just the three levels available with Levels adjustments. For example, instead of adjusting only the shadows, highlights, or midtones, you could use curves to adjust the contrast of pixels with brightness levels between 15% and 40%.

To perform a nondestructive edit with curves, do any of the following:

- Create a duplicate layer. Then choose Image, Adjustment, Curves.
- Choose Layer, New Adjustment Layer, Curves and click OK.
- In the Layers panel, click the "Create new fill or adjustment layer" icon and choose Curves from the pop-up menu.
- In the Adjustments panel, click the Curves icon.

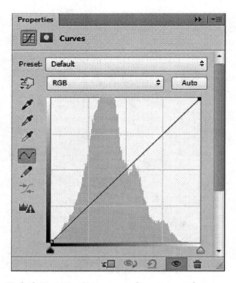

Exhibit 4-6: Curves adjustment layer options in the Properties panel

When a Curves adjustment layer is selected, the Properties panel displays the settings shown in Exhibit 4-6. By default, the curve appears as a 45° line, indicating that the output values match the input values, resulting in no change to the image.

You can click anywhere along the curve to add a point, and you can then drag that point to adjust the curve. Dragging a point straight down darkens the areas at the current input level. Dragging up brightens the image. You can drag a point away from the curve area to remove it, or you can press Alt and click Reset to return the curve to its default.

For realistic corrections, the curve should generally slant up and to the right. If the curve dips down, it reverses the tonal areas and the result looks unnatural.

Do it!

B-1:   Adjusting contrast with curves

The files for this activity are in Student Data folder **Unit 4\Topic B**.

Here's how	Here's why
1 Open Impala 2	
Save the image as **My impala 2**	(In the current topic folder.) You'll adjust contrast by using a Curves adjustment layer.
2 In the Adjustments panel, click	(The Curves icon.) To create an adjustment layer and to display the Curves options in the Properties panel. You'll create points on the curve and then modify them.
3 Click the center of the curve as shown	To create a point.
Drag the point you just created slightly below and to the right of the midpoint	To darken the image. Areas that were at 50% brightness are now at a lower brightness level on the output axis.

4 Drag the point up slightly above the midpoint

To brighten the image.

5 Click the curve to the right of the point you just created, as shown

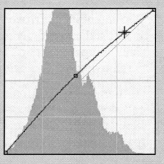

To create another point.

Drag the new point straight down to create a curve, as shown

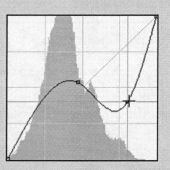

Because the curve dips down, the tonal areas are reversed, creating an unnatural appearance.

6 Click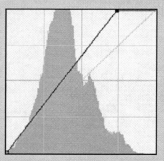

To remove the points you created and return the curve to a 45° line. Next, you'll move the top endpoint of the curve to control the highlights.

7 Drag the top endpoint of the curve to the left, as shown

To brighten the overall image. Next, you'll move the bottom endpoint to control the shadows of the image.

8   Drag the bottom endpoint of the
curve to the right, as shown

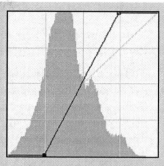

To darken the shadows.

The image now has more contrast. A steeper
curve represents more contrast because the
shadows are darker and highlights are lighter.

9   Drag the endpoints of the curve as
shown

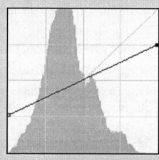

The contrast decreases, and the image looks
washed out.

Click 🔄

10 Create a midpoint and place it as
shown

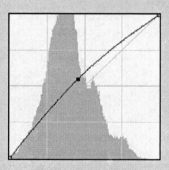

To lighten the midtones.

11 Update the image

Using curves to adjust specific tones

Explanation

You can use curves to adjust specific tonal regions of an image. To target a particular tonal region, you can estimate where to click the curve and then drag as necessary.

To more accurately target the adjustment, you can use the Targeted Adjustment tool—available in the Properties panel—to select a specific area of the image to adjust. As you move the pointer, a circle appears on the curve, indicating the brightness value of the pixel you're pointing to. You can then press Ctrl and click the image to add a point, representing that brightness level, to the curve.

You can also drag with the Targeted Adjustment tool in an image to increase or decrease the curve setting for the particular tonal range you're pointing to.

To limit an adjustment to a specific color, select a color channel from the Channel list. A new curve appears for the color channel you selected. In addition, when you're making on-image adjustments, you can press Ctrl and click the image to add a point to each individual color-channel curve.

Applying an adjustment layer to a single layer

By default, an adjustment layer affects all layers below it. However, you can specify that an adjustment layer affects only the layer directly below it. To do so, in the Properties panel, click the Clip to layer button, shown in Exhibit 4-6.

Do it!

B-2: Adjusting specific tones

Here's how	Here's why
1 In the Properties panel, press `ALT` and click **Auto**	To open the Auto Color Correction Options dialog box.
Select **Enhance Per Channel Contrast**	
Click **OK**	
2 In the Properties panel, click [icon]	(The Targeted Adjustment tool.) The pointer changes to a half-filled Eyedropper.
Move the pointer over the impala's face	
In the Properties panel, observe the circle that appears on the curve	The circle moves in relation to the Eyedropper's position—it appears at the top-right when you point to a white area, and it appears at the bottom-left when you point to a black area.

3 Point to the indicated area

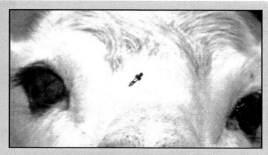

This area represents the lightest part of the image, and the highlights are blown out. You'll try to recover some detail.

Click the white area and drag down

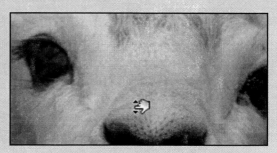

To add a point to the curve and move it down, darkening the pixels in the tonal range you selected.

4 Move the Eyedropper in the image until you find a point roughly corresponding to the indicated position on the curve

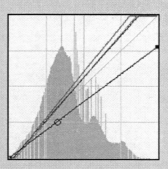

In the image, drag down slightly

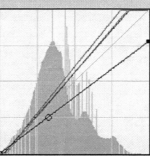

To darken the pixels in the selected tonal range, adding more contrast.

5 From the Channel list, select **Red**

Preset: Custom

Red | Auto

In the Curves display, the green and blue channel lines disappear. If the histogram is displayed in the background, it displays only the red channel.

6 Move the Eyedropper in the image until you find a point roughly corresponding to the indicated position on the curve

In the image, drag up slightly

To increase the selected tonal range.

Because this image contains more than one layer, you can specify that the adjustment layer affect only the layer directly below it, rather than all layers.

7 In the Properties panel, click

To clip the Curves adjustment layer to the layer below it in the image.

8 Update and close the image

Unit summary: Basic image adjustments

Topic A   In this topic, you used the **Auto Color Correction Options** dialog box to specify an automatic adjustment to a **Levels adjustment layer**. You also used the **target point tools** to specify an image's target highlights and shadows.

Topic B   In this topic, you used a **Curves adjustment layer** to adjust image contrast. You also manipulated curves to adjust specific tones by using the **Targeted Adjustment tool**. You also applied a **clipping mask** to an adjustment layer to apply the adjustment to only a single layer.

Independent practice activity

In this activity, you'll apply an automatic adjustment using an adjustment layer. Then you'll fine-tune the adjustment by adjusting shadows and highlights. Finally, you'll use a Curves adjustment layer to adjust specific tones.

The files for this activity are in Student Data folder **Unit 4\Unit summary**.

1 Open Overexposed building, and save it in Photoshop format as **My overexposed building**.

2 Create a Levels adjustment layer. Apply the **Enhance Brightness and Contrast** Auto adjustment. (*Hint*: Open the Auto Color Correction Options dialog box.)

3 Locate the image's shadows and highlights. Then place a shadow color sampler and a highlight color sampler.

4 Set black and white target points, using the target color values shown in Exhibit 4-7.

5 Add a Curves adjustment layer. Specify an Auto setting that you think looks best.

6 Using the Targeted Adjustment tool, drag in the image to enhance the contrast. (*Hint*: Try to find highlights, midtones, and shadows along the curve as you point in the image.)

7 Update and close the image.

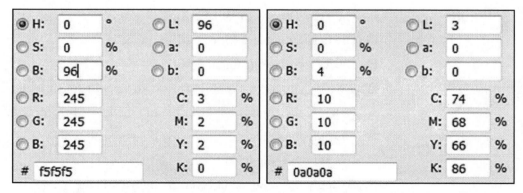

Exhibit 4-7: Target white (left) and black (right) color values for Step 4

Review questions

1 How can you perform an adjustment as a nondestructive edit? [Choose all that apply.]

A Use the commands on the Image menu and its submenus.

B Use the Adjustments panel to perform a color correction on an adjustment layer, which can be reset or deleted if necessary.

C Create a duplicate Background layer and perform destructive edits on that layer, preserving the original layer.

D Use the Color Replacement tool.

2 Which components can you modify by using a Levels adjustment layer? [Choose all that apply.]

A Highlights

B Shadows

C Blending modes

D Transparency

E Midtones

3 What does dragging the gamma slider to the left in the Levels dialog box do to the image?

A Brightens the highlights

B Darkens the shadows

C Brightens the midtones

D Darkens the midtones

4 What tool can you use to modify a Curves adjustment layer by pointing to the area in the image you want to modify and dragging?

A The Eyedropper tool.

B The Free Transform tool.

C The Content-Aware Move tool.

D The Targeted Adjustment tool.

5 Why would you use a clipping mask with an adjustment layer?

A To apply the adjustment layer to only the layer directly below it

B To apply the adjustment layer to all layers below it

C To apply the adjustment layer to all layers above it

D To apply the adjustment layer to all layers in the image

Unit 5

Repairing and retouching images

Complete this unit, and you'll know how to:

A Repair image defects by using the Red Eye, Spot Healing Brush, and Patch tools.

B Retouch images by using the Burn, Blur, Content-Aware Move, Clone Stamp, and History Brush tools.

C Remove image areas by using the Background Eraser tool and Content-Aware Fill.

D Select a painting color and use the Brush tool to paint in an image.

E Use the Filter Gallery to apply filters to a layer or selection.

Topic A: Repairing image defects

Explanation

One of the most popular uses of Photoshop is to repair defects in images. Photoshop includes a number of tools to repair defects, and many of them perform similar tasks. However, each tool, combined with its unique options, is useful for certain types of defects.

The Red Eye tool

Red eye is a common defect in digital photos, caused when the camera flash bounces off the back of a person's retinas, causing their eyes to appear red. You can use the Red Eye tool to fix such defects

When you select the Red Eye tool, you can specify its settings on the options bar, shown in Exhibit 5-1. The Pupil Size box indicates the size of the resulting pupil relative to the size of the red area. The red area is typically larger than a person's pupil, so you would specify a Pupil Size percentage of less than 100. The Darken Amount box specifies how much the resulting pupil should be darkened.

Exhibit 5-1: Red Eye tool options

To repair a red-eye defect:

1.   Select the Red Eye tool from the Tools panel group that includes the Spot Healing Brush tool.
2.   Specify Red Eye settings on the options bar.
3.   Click each affected eye to repair the red-eye effect.

Do it!

A-1: Fixing red eye

The files for this activity are in Student Data folder **Unit 5\Topic A**.

Here's how	Here's why
1 Open Red eye girl	
Save the image in Photoshop format as **My red eye girl**	In the current topic folder.
2 In the Tools panel, click and hold the Spot Healing Brush tool, as shown	
	To show the tool group.
Select the **Red Eye Tool**	
On the options bar, verify that the Pupil Size and Darken Amount settings are 50%	To use the default settings.
3 Click the eye on the left	(The girl's right eye.) To correct the red eye.
4 Click the eye on the right	(The girl's left eye.) Observe that the pupil is not quite as dark as the one in the other eye.
5 Press CTRL + Z	
6 Edit the Pupil Size box to read **75**	(On the options bar.) To increase the area affected by the Red Eye tool.
Edit the Darken Amount box to read **85**	To increase the amount of darkness for the correction.
Click the eye on the right	The eyes now match more closely.
7 Update and close the image	

The Spot Healing Brush tool

Another tool you can use to fix image imperfections is the Spot Healing Brush tool. It's useful for fixing small blemishes, such as acne on a face, dust specks or scratches in an old photograph, or other small imperfections.

To use the Spot Healing Brush tool to fix a small blemish, click the area you want to fix. The Spot Healing Brush tool samples pixels from around the area you clicked and paints them onto the area you clicked.

Rather than completely replacing the pixels with the sampled pixels, however, this tool matches the texture, lighting, transparency, and shading of the sampled pixels to the pixels you're touching up, creating a clean touchup. While you're pressing the mouse button, the area you're touching up appears to darken, but when you release the mouse button, the area blends to match the underlying image.

Source sampling types

Depending on the image and the kinds of imperfections you need to fix, you can specify different source sampling types for the Spot Healing Brush tool. With the tool selected, on the options bar, select one of the following:

- **Proximity Match** — Examines pixels around the edge of a selection,
- **Create Texture** — Creates a texture based on pixels within the selection.
- **Content-Aware** — Fills the selection based on nearby content, maintaining details such as shadows and edges.

The Healing Brush tool

The Healing Brush tool is similar to the Spot Healing Brush tool. The Spot Healing Brush tool works well for areas that are smaller than the current brush size, but for larger areas, its results often appear artificial. For fixing medium-sized or large defects, you can get better results with the Healing Brush tool.

To use the Healing Brush tool to fix an image defect, you first have to sample another image area, as you do with the Clone Stamp tool. However, while the Clone Stamp tool paints an exact copy of the sampled area, the Healing Brush Tool paints the sampled pixels and matches them to the texture of the area you're fixing, creating a clean touchup. Therefore, you can get a good result even if you sample from part of the image that is quite different from the area you're fixing.

While you're dragging over the area you want to fix, it appears discolored. When you release the mouse button, the area blends to match the underlying texture.

Do it!

A-2:   Repairing defects with the Spot Healing Brush tool

The files for this activity are in Student Data folder **Unit 5\Topic A**.

Here's how	Here's why
1 Open Tomatoes 1	
Save the image in Photoshop format as **My tomatoes 1**	In the current topic folder.
2 Zoom to 50% on the indicated area	(At the right of the image.) The tomato has some imperfections. You'll use the Spot Healing Brush tool to remove them.
3 In the Tools panel, click and hold the Red Eye tool	To show the tool group.
Select the **Spot Healing Brush Tool**	
Press ( ])	(If necessary.) To set the brush size to 20 pixels. The Brush settings on the options bar show the current brush size.
Set the brush size to **40**	
4 Observe the options bar	Type: ◯ Proximity Match ◯ Create Texture ⦿ Content-Aware The source sampling type is set to Content-Aware by default. Different types might work better for different images or imperfections.
5 Click a black spot	To remove it from the image.
6 Click or drag over each black spot on the tomato	To remove the spot or imperfection. You can drag over larger areas to repair them.
7 Update the image	

The Patch tool

Explanation

When fixing a large image defect that contrasts sharply with the surrounding area, you'll get the best results by using the Patch tool. Painting over a large area with the Healing Brush tool can be time-consuming, and the defect is often not completely removed. In addition, you can think of the Patch tool as a way to remove objects from an image.

The Patch tool is similar to the two Healing Brush tools in that it blends the texture, lighting, and shading of the sampled pixels to the pixels you're touching up, thereby creating a clean touchup. To use the Patch tool, however, you drag around the area you want to fix, similar to selecting an area with the Lasso tool. After selecting the area you want to fix, point inside the selection and drag to an area you want to sample. As you drag, you can preview the area you're sampling within the area you're fixing.

If you prefer to select the area you want to sample and drag it onto the area you want to fix, then begin by selecting Destination on the options bar.

Do it!

A-3: Repairing large defects with the Patch tool

The files for this activity are in Student Data folder **Unit 5\Topic A**.

Here's how	Here's why
1 Scroll to the bottom-right of the image	This tomato has a damaged area too large to fix with the Spot Healing Brush. But there's an undamaged tomato next to it that you can use to fix it.
2 In the Tools panel, click and hold the Spot Healing Brush tool	To show the tool group.
Select the **Patch Tool**	
3 On the options bar, from the Patch list, select **Content Aware**	Patch: Content-Aware

4 Draw a marquee around the
damaged area, as shown

5 Drag from within the marquee to
the left

To point to the area you want to use to fix the
damage. Photoshop shows what the original
selection will look like.

Release the mouse   To apply the patch.

6 Press ⌈ CTRL ⌉ + ⌈ D ⌉

7 Press ⌈ CTRL ⌉ + ⌈ 0 ⌉

Update and close the image

Topic B: Retouching images

This topic covers the following ACE exam objectives for Photoshop CS6.

#	Objective
7.1	**Working with the retouching tools**
7.1.1	Using Dodge, Burn, Smudge, Blur
7.1.2	Edge smoothing techniques
7.1.3	Using the Clone Stamp, History Brush, and Sponge
7.5	**Using the Clone Source panel**
7.5.1	Understanding how to the use the clone source tool
7.5.2	Understanding horizontal vertical offsets
7.5.3	Understanding rotation
7.5.4	Cloning images from separate documents

Enhancing image elements

Explanation

Often, you'll be working with an image that doesn't necessarily contain "defects," but one that you want to enhance by manipulating the elements within it. You can use various tools to darken and lighten specific areas, to smooth rough edges, and to clone elements.

Toning tools

You can retouch small areas by using the toning tools. Mimicking techniques used by photographers, these tools include the Dodge, Burn, and Sponge tools.

The Dodge tool lightens image areas, the Burn tool darkens image areas, and the Sponge tool increases or decreases color saturation. Each tool affects only the pixels that you drag it over.

In addition, when you select the Dodge or Burn tools, you can click the Range list on the options bar to specify whether the tool will affect shadows, midtones, or highlights. For the Sponge tool, click the options bar's Mode list to specify whether the tool will saturate or desaturate image colors. For the Dodge and Burn tools, specify an Exposure value on the options bar to control the strength of the tool's impact.

The effect of these tools is cumulative—the more you paint with them, the more pronounced their effect becomes.

The toning tools are painting tools, so they permanently change the pixels in your image. Therefore, you might want to use these tools on a duplicate layer, so you can keep the original layer in case you need to return to it later.

Do it!

B-1: Using the Burn tool to darken image areas

The files for this activity are in Student Data folder **Unit 5\Topic B**.

Here's how	Here's why
1 Open Impala 3	
Save the image as **My impala 3**	In the current topic folder.
2 Select the **Impala** layer	To preserve it from a destructive edit.
Press ⌈ CTRL ⌉ + ⌈ J ⌉	To duplicate the layer. You'll adjust the image pixels directly, so you want to keep the original layer as a backup.
3 Zoom to 100% on the indicated area	Previously, the impala was selected and copied to a new layer. Then a curves adjustment was applied to only the Impala layer, resulting in a dark streak and a sharp edge along the animal's outline. You'll use toning tools to fix this.
4 In the Tools panel, click [🔍]	The Dodge tool.
On the options bar, from the Range list, select **Shadows**	
Set the brush size to **20**	
5 Drag over the dark strip at the edge of the impala's back	To lighten that area slightly.
Continue dragging with the Dodge tool	Until the color more closely blends with the colors next to it. The effect isn't perfect, so you'll also use the Blur tool to blend the colors more.
6 Update the image	

Edge smoothing

Explanation

You might not think that you'd want to make an image blurrier or to reduce the amount of detail, but there are some situations in which it makes sense to make these adjustments to part of an image. For example, if part of an image has a very sharp edge that makes it look unnatural—perhaps because a selection was copied and pasted from another image, for example—then you might want to blur the edge slightly to make it look more natural.

The Blur tool works very simply—you just drag with it over the parts of the image you want to blur by reducing detail. At first, you might not notice much of a change. However, the more you use it, the more pronounced the effect becomes. In addition, you can specify settings on the options bar to change how the tool blurs your image.

Do it!

B-2: Smoothing edges with the Blur tool

Here's how	Here's why
1 Zoom to 100% on the indicated area	 (If necessary.) There's a sharp edge around the impala, especially along the bottom of its ear. You'll reduce the detail so that it looks less obvious.
2 In the Tools panel, click Set the brush size to **30**	
3 Drag along the bottom of the impala's ear	Until the level of detail begins to resemble the surrounding image.
4 Drag along the edge of the impala's back	By reducing detail, the Blur tool also blends adjacent colors together, making the transition between them less distinct and, at least in this case, more natural.
5 Continue dragging in the image	To reduce any sharp edges.
6 Update and close the image	

Content-Aware Move

Explanation

The Content-Aware Move tool combines the functions of several different tools and steps. If, for example, you wanted to move a selection in one part of an image to another part, you might have to select it, move it, and then use a tool such as the Clone Stamp tool to fill in the hole created when you move the selection. Instead, by using the Content-Aware Move tool, when you move a selection, Photoshop automatically fills the hole, matching it to the surrounding content.

The Content-Aware Move tool actually has two functions: moving and extending. To move an element in an image:

1 Using a selection tool, select the area you want to move. This doesn't have to be a perfect selection—Photoshop will attempt to match the areas you select to the destination.

2 Select the Content-Aware Move tool.

3 On the options bar, from the Move list, select Move.

4 Drag the selection where you want to move it.

5 Using the other healing tools, clean up the image by repairing, patching, or cloning areas that don't match.

When you move a selection, the original selection is deleted. If you want to retain the original selection, then, on the options bar, from the Move list, select Extend. This is useful for extending architectural elements, for example.

The results when using this tool will vary, and it works best when moving selections that have a uniform or consistent background.

Do it!

B-3:   Using the Content-Aware Move tool

The files for this activity are in Student Data folder **Unit 5\Topic B**.

Here's how	Here's why
1 Open Sheep 1	
Save the image as **My sheep 1**	(In the current topic folder.) You want to rearrange some elements in the image. First, you'll extend the fence at the center to the left.
2 Press (CTRL) + (0)	
3 Using the Rectangular Marquee tool, select the indicated area	
	Extend the selection to the top edge of the image; don't include the hinge on the left or the gap between the fence and the building on the right; do include the ground below the fence, but not the sheep.

4 Press CTRL + ALT + SHIFT + N	(To create a new empty layer.) Because the fence isn't perfectly straight, you might need to modify the section you're moving.
5 In the Tools panel, click and hold the Spot Healing Brush tool	
Select the **Content-Aware Move Tool**	
On the options bar, from the Mode list, select **Extend**	You'll extend the selection, leaving the original selection in place.
Verify that Sample All Layers is checked	The new layer you created is selected; you want the Content-Aware Move tool to sample the layer below it.
6 Point inside the selection, and begin dragging it left	
While dragging, hold SHIFT and move the selection to the indicated position	

You want to overlap the original selection slightly. When you release the mouse, Photoshop blends the selection into the image, attempting to match its content.

Observe the image

Where the two sections meet, they don't line up perfectly. Before you extend the fence farther, you'll fix this.

7 Press `CTRL` + `T`

Hold `CTRL` + `SHIFT` and drag
the bottom-right handle up
slightly

So that the bottom edges of the fence sections
line up.

Press `↵ ENTER`

Press `CTRL` + `D`

8 Make a selection, as shown

It should be wide enough to fill the remaining
area to the left.

9 Press
   `CTRL` + `ALT` + `SHIFT` + `N`

To create a new empty layer.

Using the Content-Aware Move
tool, drag the selection to the left

To extend the fence to the left edge.

10 Press `CTRL` + `D` and observe
    the image

This time, the bottoms of the fences should have
lined up pretty well. Now you want to move a
sheep.

11 Using the Lasso tool, select the
    indicated area

The big sheep at the right of the image.

12 Press (SHIFT) + (J)   To select the Content-Aware Move tool.

On the options bar, from the Mode list, select **Move**

Press
(CTRL) + (ALT) + (SHIFT) + (N)

Drag the sheep to the indicated position

When you release the mouse, Photoshop fills in the original selection, matching the surrounding image. The area around the sheep you moved, however, needs some work. You can use the Clone Stamp tool to fix it.

13 Press (CTRL) + (D)

Update the image

The Clone Stamp tool

Explanation

You can use the Clone Stamp tool to sample part of an image and paint it in other parts of the image. (*Sampling* copies the pixels from one area of an image so that they can be applied to another area.) For example, you could use the Clone Stamp tool to sample a cloud and paint it over an airplane, in effect removing the airplane from the image.

To use the Clone Stamp tool to clone part of an image:

1   In the Tools panel, select the Clone Stamp tool.
2   On the options bar, specify the tool settings you want.
3   Press Alt and click the part of the image you want to duplicate.
4   Point to the part of the image where you want to add the sampled image area, and drag to paint the sampled area.

As you drag, a crosshair appears as a reference point to show the part of the image you're sampling from. As you paint, the reference point moves to clone different parts of the image. If you point to another part of the image and begin painting, the reference point starts out at a new position, which is a set distance from the pointer.

If you want the reference point to always begin where you last pressed Alt and clicked, no matter where you begin painting, clear the Aligned box on the options bar.

The Clone Source panel

For greater control over the areas you clone, you can use the Clone Source panel, shown in Exhibit 5-2. For example, you can set up to five sampling points—each from a different image open in Photoshop, if you'd like—by clicking a Clone Source button and then selecting an area to sample. You can scale and rotate each clone source by editing the associated boxes on the right side of the Clone Source panel. You can also specify the Offset values if, for example, you want to paint a specific location relative to the sampled area.

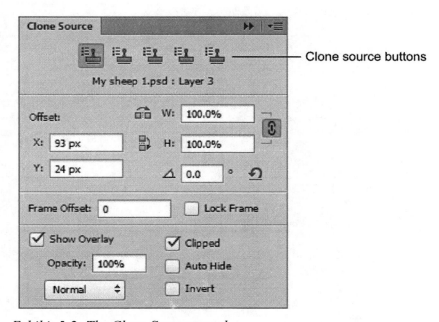

Exhibit 5-2: The Clone Source panel

You can also use the Clone Source panel to sample areas from other open images. You could, for example, clone an area in one image and paint the sampled area into another image, using the Clone Source panel to keep track of which images you've sampled.

It's sometimes difficult to know exactly which part of the image you'll be cloning when you position the Clone Stamp tool. To make it easier to visualize, you can check Show Overlay. When you do, an overlay of the original image appears. When you move the mouse, the overlay shows what part of the image you'll clone when you paint with the Clone Stamp tool.

Do it!

B-4: Cloning image areas

The files for this activity are in Student Data folder **Unit 5\Topic B**.

Here's how	Here's why
1 In the Tools panel, click [icon]	(The Clone Stamp tool.) You'll clean up the area around the sheep you moved by cloning other image areas.
2 Choose **Window**, **Clone Source**	To display the Clone Source panel.
3 On the options bar, click as shown [options bar image: stamp tool, 50, Mode: Normal]	
	To display the Brush Preset picker.
Set the brush size to **40**	The brush size should be small enough for you to do precise cloning, but large enough so you don't have to use too many strokes.
Set the Hardness to **75%** [Size: 40 px / Hardness: 75% sliders]	
	To specify that the tool use some feathering when you paint with it, since the area you're painting in doesn't have hard edges.
Press (↵ ENTER)	To confirm the settings and close the Brush Preset picker.
4 Verify that **Aligned** is checked	On the options bar.
From the Sample list, select **All Layers**	The image contains multiple layers; clearing this option will treat it as if it were a single layer.
5 Zoom to 100% on the sheep you moved	Photoshop wasn't able to match the area around it exactly with the surrounding content.

6 Press ⟨ALT⟩ and click as shown

To sample the area just to the left of the sheep.

Position the pointer as shown

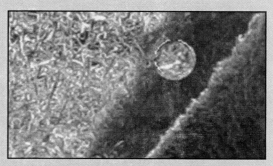

The overlay shows what part of the image will appear when you paint with the tool.

Use short strokes to paint over the shadow, as shown

To clone the area you sampled, removing the shadow from the image. Whenever you release the mouse button, the overlay updates to reflect the changes you've made in the image.

At the top of the sheep, you realize you want to clone the area above the shadow, not to the left.

7 In the Clone Source panel, click the second Clone Source button

My sheep 1.psd : Layer 3

You'll sample another area in the image, but you also want to save the first sampled area in case you need to use it again.

Sample the indicated area above the sheep

Press Alt and click.

Paint over the shadow

To remove it from the image by cloning the sampled area.

8 Create a new clone source for the right side of the sheep

In the Clone Source panel, click the third Clone Source button. Then Alt+click the area you want to sample.

Because the area you want to clone over is larger, you might reach the edge of the cloned area. You'll specify that the Clone Stamp tool not keep the clone source aligned.

On the options bar, clear **Aligned**

Every time you release and then click the mouse button again, the clone source returns to the original location.

Clone over the shadow on the right and underneath the sheep

The shadow in the original area of the image should extend underneath the sheep.

9 Create a fourth clone source at the
   bottom of the sheep

   Clone over the remaining shadow

10 Close the Clone Source panel

11 Press (CTRL) + (0)   To fit the entire image in the window.

   Update the image

The History panel and the Art History Brush tool

Explanation

You can paint in an image with the History Brush tool or the Art History Brush tool.
Rather than painting with solid color as you do with the Brush tool, however, you'll be
painting with pixels from a state in the History panel.

History panel states and snapshots

The History panel records, by default, the 20 most recent actions you've performed in
Photoshop. Each saved action is called a *state*. As you perform additional steps, older
states are deleted from the History panel.

If you want to save the current image state so that it remains in the History panel no
matter how many additional steps you perform during the work session, you can save it
as a snapshot. A *snapshot* is a saved image state that appears at the top of the History
panel. When you close the image, however, snapshots are cleared from the History
panel.

To save the current image state as a named snapshot:

1 In the History panel, click the state that you want to save as a snapshot.

2 Open the New Snapshot dialog box by doing either of the following:

   • Press Alt and click the Create new snapshot button at the bottom of the
      History panel. (If you click this button without pressing Alt, the new
      snapshot is automatically named Snapshot 1. You can then double-click the
      name to change it.)

   • From the History panel menu, choose New Snapshot.

3 In the Name box, enter the name you want.

4 From the From list, select an option to specify whether the snapshot includes all
   document layers, the current layer, or all layers merged to a single layer.

5 Click OK.

Painting with the History Brush and Art History Brush tools

The History Brush tool paints pixels into an image exactly as they appear in the specified state or snapshot in the History panel. The Art History Brush tool paints the pixels from the specified history state but with a simulated painting style that you choose.

To paint pixels from a history state into the current image:

    1   In the History panel, click to the left of the state or snapshot whose pixels you want to paint into the image.

    2   Select the History Brush tool or the Art History Brush tool.

    3   If you're using the Art History Brush tool, select a Style from the options bar.

    4   Drag in the image to paint pixels from the specified history state.

Do it!   **B-5: Painting with the History Brush**

Here's how	Here's why
1 Press CTRL + 0	You decide you want the sheep back in its original position, while also keeping the one you moved. You can quickly paint it back in.
2 In the Tools panel, click	The History Brush tool.
3 In the dock, click	To display the History panel.
Scroll to the top of the panel	Sheep 1.psd
	By default, the first state is selected. This is the original image.
4 Create a new empty layer	(Press Ctrl+Alt+Shift+N.) In which to "paint back" the origial content.
5 Set the brush size to **300**	
Paint over in the image over the grassy area	Where the sheep originally was. As you paint, the selected history state is painted into the image.
6 Update and close the image	

Topic C: Removing image areas

Explanation   There are several ways to eliminate objects or areas from an image in Photoshop. You can use the Spot Healing Brush, Healing Brush, and Patch tools to remove defects, but you might want to remove larger or more complex areas for which these tools wouldn't be as effective. You can use the Background Eraser tool to selectively erase pixels surrounding an object so that only the object you want remains. For complex foreground areas that appear over multicolored backgrounds, the Background Eraser tool is easier to use than a selection tool and typically yields better results. In addition, you can use a Content-Aware Fill to automatically fill a selection you've deleted with the background from the surrounding image.

Preparing images before erasing the background

If you plan to erase a background so you can display the foreground area over a new background, there are a few steps you should take before you begin:

1   Add the new background you want to use as a new layer so that you can see how the image looks as you erase the original background. Seeing the new background will help you blend the edges of the foreground with it.

2   Make a copy of the layer containing the background you plan to erase so you can return to it if you erase too much and need to start over.

3   Use the Eraser tool or the selection tools to remove the sections of the background that can be easily removed without deleting whatever part of the foreground you're trying to isolate. Then you can erase the more difficult areas of the background by using the Background Eraser tool.

Do it!

C-1:   Preparing an image before removing a background

The files for this activity are in Student Data folder **Unit 5\Topic C**.

Here's how	Here's why
1 Open Sheep 2	
Save the image as **My sheep 2**	In the current topic folder.
2 Open Lion 1	
3 Choose **Window**, **Arrange**, **2-up Vertical**	
4 In the Layers panel, drag the Background layer into the My sheep 2 image	
Close the Lion 1 image	
5 Resize and position Layer 1 as shown	

Use the Free Transform command.

6 Hide the Moved sheep layer	

In the Layers panel, click its visibility icon.

7 Zoom to 50% on the lion

In the Tools panel, click   The Eraser tool.

Set the brush size to **300**

Erase most of the area around the lion

8 Reduce the brush size to **100**

Erase more of the area around the lion, but keep a region around it

You can use the Background Eraser tool to erase the background around detailed edges.

9 Update the image

Erasing a complex background

Explanation

You can use the Background Eraser tool to erase background pixels with precision while retaining complex foreground details. To erase a background with the Background Eraser tool:

1 Select the Background Eraser tool, which is in the same tool group as the Eraser tool.

2 On the options bar, use the Brush Preset picker to specify a brush size.

3 On the options bar, specify the sampling type you want to use.

- Click the *Sampling: Continuous* icon to erase all pixels you drag across that match the color at the center of the pointer as you drag. This option works well for backgrounds that contain many colors, because the colors that are erased can change constantly as you drag over them.

- Click the *Sampling: Once* icon to erase only colors that match the color that was under the pointer when you began dragging. This option works well when the background is made up of a small number of colors. You can stop dragging and begin in a new location to start erasing a different color.

- Click the *Sampling: Background Swatch* icon to erase only colors that match the current background color, shown in the Background color box in the Tools panel. This option works well for images with a single background color.

4 On the options bar, from the Limits list, select a limits mode.

- Select *Discontiguous* to erase all instances of the sampled color located below the pointer as you drag.

- Select *Contiguous* to erase only instances of the sampled color that are connected to one another.

- Select *Find Edges* to erase connected areas of the sampled color while better preserving the sharpness of shape edges.

5 On the options bar, in the Tolerance box, specify a value to define how similar to the sampled color other areas must be to be erased. A low tolerance erases only areas very similar to the sampled color, and a high tolerance erases a broader range of colors.

6 On the options bar, select Protect Foreground Color to ensure that you won't erase colors matching the current foreground color.

7 Drag over the areas containing the background that you want to erase.

Do it!

C-2:   Removing a complex background

Here's how	**Here's why**
1 From the Eraser tool group, select the **Background Eraser Tool**	
Set the brush size to **30**	
On the options bar, click	The Sampling: Once icon.
2 Press (ALT) and click the indicated area	
	To temporarily access the Eyedropper tool and sample this color as the foreground color. You'll tell Photoshop not to erase this color.
On the options bar, check **Protect Foreground Color**	To prevent accidental erasure of the lion.
3 Point to the indicated area	
	The location of the crosshair when you click the mouse button is the sample color that will be erased.
Paint around the lion's head	
	The background is erased, but the lion isn't because it's not the color that you sampled.

4 Sample an area above the lion's back

Remove the background up to the lion's tail

Here, the background color is much closer to the color of the tip of the lion's tail.

5 Zoom to 100% on the lion's tail

Sample the black color from the tip of the lion's tail

(Press Alt and click the color.) To make it the protected foreground color.

Carefully paint around the lion's tail

To remove the background. You likely won't be able to remove all of it. You could use the Eraser tool with a small brush size to erase the rest.

6 Sample the foreground color

To make it the color of the lion

Continue painting to remove the background

7   Press ⟨ALT⟩ and click Layer 1's visibility icon   (To hide all but that layer.) To better see any remaining areas you need to erase.

Using the Eraser tool, erase the remaining areas

Because the remaining areas blend with the image background, you don't need to erase it entirely.

Press ⟨ALT⟩ and click Layer 1's visibility icon   To show the layers you hid.

8   Press ⟨CTRL⟩ + ⟨O⟩

Update the image

Content-Aware Fill

Explanation   If your image contains an object or area you want to remove completely, you can try doing so by using the Clone Stamp tool to sample surrounding areas. However, some images contain complex backgrounds that make using the Clone Stamp tool difficult.

Content-Aware Fill automatically fills a selection with nearby content. To use Content-Aware Fill:

1   Select the area you want to replace with the surrounding content (for example, a person standing in front of a background).
2   Choose Edit, Fill, or press Delete or Backspace, to open the Fill dialog box.
3   From the Use list, select Content-Aware.
4   Click OK.

If the results aren't perfect, you can touch them up with other tools, such as the Healing Brush, Patch, and Clone Stamp tools.

C-3: Using Content-Aware Fill to delete a selection

The files for this activity are in Student Data folder **Unit 5\Topic C**.

Here's how	Here's why
1 Select the Lasso tool	You'll remove a sheep from the image.
Draw a selection around the indicated sheep	
2 Select the **Background** layer	This is the layer the sheep is on.
3 Press (← BACKSPACE)	To open the Fill dialog box.
In the Use list, verify that **Content-Aware** is selected	
Click **OK**	
	To close the dialog box. Photoshop fills the selection.
4 Press (CTRL) + (D)	To deselect the selection. If there's a slight distortion, you could use the Patch tool or the Clone Stamp tool to fix it.
5 Update and close the image	

Topic D: Painting

This topic covers the following ACE exam objectives for Photoshop CS6.

#	Objective
7.9	**Selecting color**
7.9.3	Adjusting colors that are out of gamut

Foreground and background colors

Explanation

When you use a painting tool, the color you apply is the color shown in the Foreground color box in the Tools panel. When you erase pixels on the Background layer, you're actually painting with the color shown in the Background color box in the Tools panel.

By default, the foreground color is black and the background color is white. You can change the foreground and background colors by using the Color Picker, the Color panel, or the Swatches panel.

The Color Picker

To choose a foreground or background color by using the Color Picker, click either the Foreground or Background color box in the Tools panel. Then, in the Color Picker dialog box, click in the large color box to select a color, as shown in Exhibit 5-3. You can change the hue shown in the color box by dragging the hue slider up or down along the color ramp. You can also enter specific color values, in several color models.

If the color you specify can't be reproduced by CMYK printing, an out-of-gamut warning icon appears next to the color. Clicking the gamut-warning icon selects the closest in-gamut color.

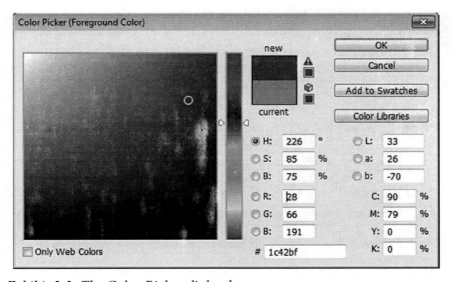

Exhibit 5-3: The Color Picker dialog box

The Color panel

You can use the Color panel to specify the foreground and background colors. To select a foreground color, click within the color ramp along the bottom of the panel. To select a background color, press Alt and click the color ramp.

By clicking the color ramp, however, you can select only in-gamut colors (colors reproducible by CMYK printing). To select any color, either drag the color sliders or enter values in the color boxes next to the sliders. If you specify an out-of-gamut color, a gamut-warning icon appears next to the color, as shown in Exhibit 5-4. Clicking the warning icon selects the closest in-gamut color.

To specify a color in a different color model, select it from the Color panel menu.

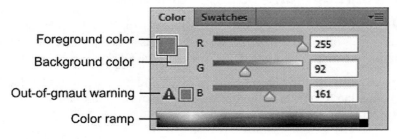

Exhibit 5-4: The Color panel

The Swatches panel

You can also select a foreground color by clicking a swatch in the Swatches panel, shown in Exhibit 5-5. To select a background color, press Ctrl and click a swatch.

To add a new color to the Swatches panel:

1   Specify the color you want to use as the foreground color.
2   Point to an empty space at the bottom of the Swatches panel. When the pointer appears as a bucket, click to open the Color Swatch Name dialog box.
3   Enter a name and click OK.

If you want to remove a swatch from the Swatches panel, press Alt and click the swatch you want to remove. When you press Alt and point to a swatch, the pointer appears as a pair of scissors, indicating that clicking will cut the swatch from the panel.

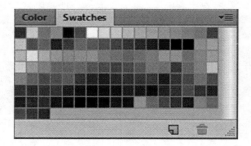

Exhibit 5-5: The Swatches panel

Do it!

D-1:   Specifying foreground and background colors

The files for this activity are in Student Data folder **Unit 5\Topic D**.

Here's how	Here's why
1 Open Sheep 3	
Save the image as **My sheep 3**	In the current topic folder.
2 Click the **Swatches** panel	It's part of the Color panel group.
Click a blue swatch	To change the foreground color to blue.
Observe the Foreground color box in the Tools panel	The box indicates that blue is now the foreground color.
Press CTRL and click a green swatch	To change the background color to green.
3 Click the **Color** panel	You'll add a color by using this panel.
In the color ramp, click a purple color, as shown	

To select a purple foreground color.

Press ALT and click a yellow color in the color ramp	To select a yellow background color. Next, you'll change the foreground color by specifying it numerically.
4 In the Color panel, drag the R slider all the way to the right	To a value of 255. This adds pure red to the foreground color.
5 Observe the out-of-gamut warning icon	

Click ⚠ or the color next to it	To change the foreground color to the closest printable color. The amount of red is reduced slightly.

The Eyedropper tool

Explanation

Another way to specify the foreground or background color is to sample a color from within an image by using the Eyedropper tool. You can click an image to select the foreground color, or press Alt and click to select the background color. You can also drag through the image until the Foreground or Background color indicator shows the color you want.

By default, using the Eyedropper tool to click within an image selects the color of the pixel you click. However, even in an area of color that appears fairly flat, you might find a variety of pixel colors. You can specify that the Eyedropper tool should generate a color by combining the colors of the pixels located around the pixel you click. To do so, display the Sample Size list on the options bar and select an option indicating the area you want to sample from.

When you use the Eyedropper tool, a color ring appears around it in the image, as shown in Exhibit 5-6. As you drag, the bottom of the ring indicates the original color you sampled, and the top of the ring indicates the color you're pointing to. This feature enables you to compare two similar colors to see which one you'd prefer to sample.

Exhibit 5-6: Sampling a color with the Eyedropper tool

Do it!   **D-2:   Sampling colors with the Eyedropper tool**

Here's how	**Here's why**
1 In the Tools panel, click	The Eyedropper tool.
2 In the image, click the lion's back	To sample the color and designate it as the foreground color.
3 Press (ALT) and click a sheep	To sample the color and designate it as the background color.
	The colors of the sheep vary, so you'll drag across one of them to find the color you want.
4 Press (ALT) and drag across the sheep on the right	
5 As you drag, observe the Background color indicator	(In the Tools panel.) The Background color indicator shows the colors you drag across.
Observe the color ring	
	The bottom of the ring indicates the color you originally clicked on, while the top indicates the color you're currently pointing to.
Continue dragging until you find the background color you want	When you release the mouse, Photoshop will use the color you're currently pointing to—i.e., the color at the top of the color ring.

Brush and Pencil tool options

Explanation

You can paint in a Photoshop image by using the Brush tool or the Pencil tool. The Pencil tool applies color with a hard edge, while the Brush tool can apply color with either a hard or soft edge. Dragging the Brush or Pencil tool applies the current foreground color to the image.

For maximum flexibility, you should create a blank layer for painting so that you won't replace any image pixels. Then you can modify or remove the color you painted without affecting the original image pixels. You can also adjust the layer's blending mode and opacity to change how the painted color appears over the pixels in underlying layers.

You can apply a blending mode directly to the brush by selecting an option from the Mode list on the options bar. Unlike blending modes applied to layers, a blending mode applied to a brush blends with pixels on the current layer instead of pixels in the underlying layers.

Before painting, specify the brush size and brush type by using the Brush Preset picker on the options bar, shown in Exhibit 5-7. To specify the brush width, drag the Size slider or enter a number in the corresponding box. Scroll through the list of brush types and sizes, and click the one you want. When you begin painting, the Brush Preset picker will close, or you can close it by clicking the triangle on the options bar or by pressing Enter.

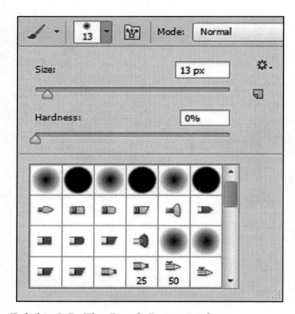

Exhibit 5-7: The Brush Preset picker

After selecting the brush size and type, you can customize the brush settings by using the Brush panel, shown in Exhibit 5-8.

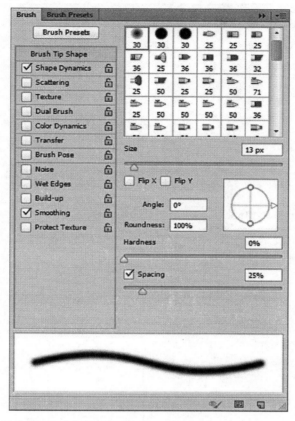

Exhibit 5-8: The Brush panel

The HUD Color Picker

When you're painting, you might find it easier to select a color without having to open a separate panel or the Color Picker. You can do so by using the HUD Color Picker. ("HUD" stands for "heads-up display.") With a painting tool selected, press Shift+Alt and right-click anywhere in the image to display the HUD Color Picker, shown in Exhibit 5-9. Drag to select a hue and shade, as you would in the regular Color Picker. The color you select becomes the new foreground color.

Exhibit 5-9: The HUD Color Picker

D-3: Painting in an image

Here's how	Here's why
1 In the Layers panel, select the **Lion** layer	You'll create a layer, and you want it to be on top of the others.
Press (CTRL) + (SHIFT) + (N)	To open the New Layer dialog box.
Edit the Name to **Paint**	
Click **OK**	You'll use the Brush tool to paint on the fence.
2 Zoom to 50% on the fence at the top-left of the image	
3 In the Tools panel, click	The Brush tool.
On the options bar, click as shown	To open the Brush Preset picker.
From the list, select the indicated option	The Charcoal Large Smear brush.
Press (↵ ENTER)	To close the Brush Preset picker.
4 Drag the Brush tool in the image	To experiment with the brush. It doesn't look the way you'd like it to.
Undo the drag	(Press Ctrl+Z.) You'll adjust the Brush tool's settings.

5	Choose **Window**, **Brush**	To open the Brush panel.
	Select **Shape Dynamics**	To display the Shape Dynamics settings.
	Drag the Angle Jitter slider to the right and observe the brush preview	Increasing the Angle Jitter setting makes the angles of the brush more uneven.
	Set the Size Jitter value to **100%**	Painting on a fence would produce an uneven effect.
	Check **Wet Edges**	
	Minimize the panel	
6	Set the brush size to **20**	
7	Press ⌈ALT⌉ and click the lion's back	To sample a dark orange color.
	Using the Brush tool, paint **Pangaea Zoo** in the image, as shown	

8	In the Layers panel, click as shown	

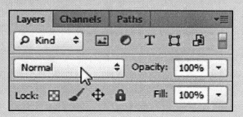

	Select **Color Burn**	To apply a blending effect to the layer.
9	Press ⌈CTRL⌉ + ⌈0⌉	
	Update and close the image	

Topic E: Using filters

Explanation

You can apply effects to an image by applying Photoshop's *filters*. Filters modify the current layer or selection with effects that range from subtle image touchups, to lighting effects, to extreme special effects that completely change the image's appearance. Filters permanently change the image pixels, and you can apply multiple filters to generate a nearly limitless variety of effects.

The Filter Gallery

Many of the filters in the Filter menu open the Filter Gallery, which is a dialog box you can use to specify and preview the effects of one or more filters. You can also open the Filter Gallery by choosing Filter, Filter Gallery. The Filter Gallery is divided into three panes, as shown in Exhibit 5-10. The left pane shows a preview of how the filter or filters you're applying will affect your image. The middle pane lists several filter categories, with the current filter selected. The right pane displays settings for the selected filter.

Exhibit 5-10: The Filter Gallery

Effect layers

In the Filter Gallery's right pane, the name of the current filter appears as an effect layer. Effect layers are useful when you want to apply multiple filters to an image, because the order in which you apply the filters affects how they change your image. You can use the Filter Gallery's effect layers to preview and experiment with the order in which you apply filters.

To add and experiment with multiple effect layers:

1 In the Filter Gallery dialog box, click the New effect layer icon at the bottom of the right pane. The first effect layer will be duplicated.

2 Select a filter in the middle pane to apply it to the new effect layer.

3 After you create multiple effect layers, you can drag them up or down to change the order in which they're applied, and preview how this changes the cumulative effect of the filters.

You can also click the eye icon next to each effect layer to hide its impact in the preview.

If you want to remove an effect layer, select it and click the Delete effect layer icon.

The Fade command

After you apply a filter, you can change how it affects the image by choosing Edit, Fade <filter name>. In the Fade dialog box, you can specify an opacity value and a blending mode to adjust how the filter affects the image, as though the filter existed on its own layer. You can apply the Fade command immediately after applying a filter. You can also use the Fade command to apply opacity and blending mode settings immediately after using a painting tool, using an erasing tool, or applying a color adjustment.

Do it!

E-1: Applying filters

The files for this activity are in Student Data folder **Unit 5\Topic E**.

Here's how	Here's why
1 Open Zoo flyer 1	
Save the image as **My zoo flyer 1**	In the current topic folder.
2 Choose **Filter, Filter Gallery...**	To open the Filter Gallery dialog box.
Press CTRL + 0	
3 Click **Artistic**	▷ 📁 Artistic ▷ 📁 Brush Strokes ▷ 📁 Distort ▷ 📁 Sketch ▷ 📁 Stylize ▷ 📁 Texture
Click the **Rough Pastels** filter	The preview updates to show the filter applied to the image.

4 In the right pane, set the Stroke Length value to **40**

Set the Stroke Detail value to **5**

From the Texture list, select **Burlap**

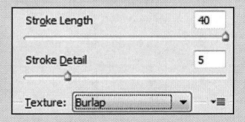

5 At the bottom of the right pane, click 🔲

(The New effect layer icon.) To create a duplicate of the Rough Pastels effect layer. You'll replace the top copy with a different filter to combine their effects.

6 In the middle pane, expand the Brush Strokes category

In the Brush Strokes category, select **Angled Strokes**

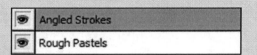

The Angled Strokes effect layer appears above the Rough Pastels effect layer, and the preview shows the impact of both filters.

Set the Sharpness value to **6**

7 Next to the Rough Pastels effect layer, click 👁

To hide the effect so you can preview the Angled Strokes filter by itself.

Show the Rough Pastels effect layer

To display the effect of the two filters together.

8 Drag the Angled Strokes effect layer below the Rough Pastels effect layer

To preview how they affect the image when applied in the reverse order.

9 Click **OK**

To apply the filters to the image.

10 Update and close the image

Unit summary: Repairing and retouching images

Topic A   In this topic, you used the **Red Eye tool** to repair a red-eye effect. You also used the **Spot Healing Brush tool** and **Patch tool** to remove image defects.

Topic B   In this topic, you retouched an image by using the **Burn** and **Blur** tools to fix problems introduced by a previous adjustment. You also used the **Content-Aware Move tool** and the **Clone Stamp tool** to extend and duplicate image elements. Finally, you used the **History Brush tool** to paint in an element from an earlier state.

Topic C   In this topic, you used the **Background Eraser tool** to erase complex background areas. You also learned how to remove an object by using **Content-Aware Fill** to fill a selection with nearby areas.

Topic D   In this topic, you used the **Color panel** and the **Swatches** panel to specify foreground and background colors. You also used the **Eyedropper tool** to sample image colors. Finally, you specified **Brush tool** settings and painted in an image.

Topic E   In this topic, you used the Filter Gallery to apply **filters** to a layer.

Independent practice activity

In this activity, you'll repair and retouch an image using various tools. You'll also remove an element from an image. In addition, you'll paint with colors sampled from an image. Finally, you'll apply a filter.

The files for this activity are in Student Data folder **Unit 5\Unit summary**.

1 Open Apples 4, and save the image as **My apples 4**.

2 Use the Patch tool to remove the stickers from the apples. (*Hint*: Zoom in close, and make the selections as small as possible.)

3 Using the Clone Stamp tool, repair any areas where problems were introduced by the use of the Patch tool.

4 Remove the background, so that your image resembles that in Exhibit 5-11. (*Hint*: Experiment with different options to see which work best.)

5 Using Content-Aware Fill, remove the chalk writing from the chalkboard. Use other tools if necessary. (*Hint*: After making a selection, use the Edit, Fill command.)

6 Create a new layer. Using the Brush tool, paint **Apples** on the chalkboard. Experiment with different brush presets, settings in the Brush panel, and blending modes.

7 Apply different filters to each image layer. Make sure the image is recognizable and that the word "Apples" can be read.

8 Update and close the image.

Exhibit 5-11: The My apples 4 image after Step 4

Review questions

1 How can you choose a different brush diameter and hardness when you're using the Brush tool to paint?

A On the options bar, open the Brush Preset picker and select a brush type.

B On the options bar, select an option from the Mode list.

C In the Tools panel, select a different brush.

D In the Tools panel, double-click the Brush tool; then select a brush type and click OK.

2 Which tool creates a duplicate of a sampled area when you paint in another area?

A The Spot Healing Brush tool

B The Patch tool

C The Clone Stamp tool

D The Healing Brush tool

3 Which of these tools do you use without sampling an image area first?

A The Spot Healing Brush tool

B The Patch tool

C The Clone Stamp tool

D The Healing Brush tool

4 To set the foreground color to a color within an image, you should click the image with the _____ tool.

5 True or false? For maximum flexibility when painting, you should create a new blank layer before using the Brush tool.

6 Which tool is most effective at isolating a complex foreground object that appears over a multicolored background?

   A The Background Eraser tool

   B The Magnetic Lasso tool

   C The Eraser tool

   D The Magic Wand tool

7 You have an image of a model standing in front of a brick wall, and you want to eliminate the model. You've tried using the Clone Stamp tool and the Patch tool without success. How can you do this?

8 The Clone Source panel would be useful for which of the following situations?

   A You want to clone an area in an image but paint it in at a different angle.

   B You want to clone several different areas in an image and save the clone sources.

   C You want to clone an area from one image to paint into another.

   D All of the above.

9 True or false? A filter doesn't permanently change pixel colors; you can change or eliminate the effect at any point after applying it.

10 When you're painting with the Brush tool, how can you specify that the brush strokes you apply should interact with the existing pixels on the current layer, such as by darkening or lightening them?

   A On the options bar, from the Mode list, select a blending mode.

   B Press Alt as you paint in the image.

   C Press Ctrl as you paint in the image.

   D Press Shift as you paint in the image.

11 In which dialog box can you experiment with applying multiple filters at once?

   A The Levels dialog box

   B The Layer Style dialog box

   C The Maximum Filter dialog box

   D The Filter Gallery dialog box

Unit 6

Resizing images

Complete this unit, and you'll know how to:

A Determine an image's resolution, and resize images with and without changing their resolution.

B Change an image's canvas size by using the Crop tool and the Canvas Size dialog box.

Topic A: Image resolution

Explanation One of the most important factors in determining the quality of a raster image designated for print use is its *image resolution*. An image's resolution measures the number of image pixels per inch (ppi).

Image quality

If an image's resolution is low, it has fewer pixels per inch, resulting in larger pixels. If an image's pixels are large enough that they're individually visible, the image appears jagged and block. When pixels are large enough that viewers can see their square shape, the image is described as *pixelated*. An image with a higher resolution has more pixels per inch, resulting in smaller pixels that produce a smoother image.

Image quality and file size

The number of pixels that make up an image determines its file size. Therefore, it's important to find a resolution that balances image quality and file size.

Most images destined for print should use a resolution of about 300 ppi. You can use a resolution a bit higher or lower, but lowering resolution too much can cause pixelation, and increasing it too much might significantly increase file size with little or no improvement in image quality. The larger an image's file size, the longer it will take to print or transfer the image, so you should keep images as small as possible while maintaining image quality.

Printer resolution is different from screen resolution. It is measured in dots per inch (dpi), not the screen metric of pixels per inch (ppi). Printer resolution is typically much higher than the resolution of the images being printed. Printer dots must be very tiny because the printer creates many dots of each ink color, with varying space between them, to create variations in shading. For example, to create gray, a printer uses many tiny black ink dots spaced in a pattern. You don't see the pattern itself because the dots are so small, but you perceive it as the color gray. This process of emulating shades of color with a high-resolution pattern of dots is called *halftoning*.

So, while a printer might have a resolution of 2400 dpi in order to create a smooth halftone, you need to send it an image with up to only 300 ppi. One image pixel color is printed by several printer dots. The file size of a 2400 ppi image would be several times larger than necessary.

However, for printing Bitmap-mode images (those using only pure white and black pixels), you should use an image resolution comparable to that of the printer, up to 1200 ppi (typically no lower than 800 ppi). Because there are no shades of gray in a bitmap image to soften the edges between black and white areas, a harsh, jagged border will be visible at lower resolutions.

File size and layers

An image's file size is determined by the number of pixels in the image, so adding layers to an image increases file size. However, when you save a Photoshop image in another file format, the image is typically flattened to a single layer. (That's why it's important to keep a copy of the original image in Photoshop's native PSD format, so you can return to it for future modifications if necessary.) When you flatten an image to a single layer of pixels, its file size decreases.

Pixel dimensions for Web images

When you display an image in a Web browser, the image automatically appears at the viewer's monitor resolution, which is typically 72 ppi or 96 ppi. The factors that determine the size of a Web image in a browser window are its width and height in pixels (pixel dimensions). The image resolution in pixels per inch doesn't matter—the "per inch" refers only to how many pixels appear in one inch when the image is printed. For example, a 70px × 70px image with a resolution of 100 ppi will appear at the same size in a Web browser as will a 70px × 70px image with a resolution of 25 ppi.

Viewing image-size data

There are several techniques you can use to view information on an image's resolution, dimensions, and file size.

- To see an approximation of how an image will appear when printed, choose View, Print Size. (Note that this doesn't display the image at the actual size it will print, but rather at a size based on the dimensions and resolution of your monitor.)

- To see how large an image will appear when viewed in a Web browser, choose View, Actual Pixels.

- To see an image's file size, click the Document statistics arrow on the status bar and select Document Sizes from the list. The status bar displays the file size based on the image being flattened, followed by the file size based on all current layers.

- To see an image's dimensions and resolution, click the Document statistics arrow on the status bar and select Document Dimensions from the list. You can also just click the Document statistics box.

- Choose View, Rulers to display horizontal and vertical rulers along the image's top and left edges. You can right-click either ruler to select a different unit of measure.

If you want to know the length of a specific element in an image, you can use the Ruler tool, which is contained in the group with the Eyedropper tool. With the Ruler tool selected, drag between two points in an image. The options bar displays the line's length and angle.

You can also use the Ruler tool to straighten an image. To do so, drag in the image across a horizontal or vertical element—for example, the horizon, if it is askew in the image. Then, on the options bar, click Straighten Layer.

Do it!

A-1: Viewing an image's resolution

The files for this activity are in Student Data folder **Unit 6\Topic A**.

Here's how	Here's why
1 Open Market flyer 4	
Save the image as **My market flyer 4**	
2 On the status bar, click as shown	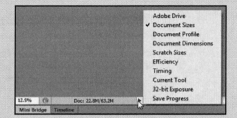
	To display the Document statistics list.
Select **Document Dimensions**	To display the image's dimensions and resolution on the status bar.
3 From the Document statistics list, select **Document Sizes**	To display the file size of the flattened image, followed by the file size of the layered image. The image with all layers is almost three times as large as the flattened version.
4 Point to the Document statistics box, and hold down the mouse button	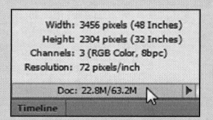
	To observe that the image dimensions are 48" × 32" but at only 72 ppi resolution.
5 Choose **View, Print Size**	To preview the image at the size at which it would print, if printed at full size.
6 Choose **View, Actual Pixels**	To preview the image at the size at which it would appear in a Web browser, if not automatically resized.
7 Choose **View, Fit on Screen**	To adjust the magnification so you can see the entire image in the Photoshop window.

Resizing without resampling

Explanation

You can use Photoshop's Image, Image Size command to change an image's dimensions or resolution. For example, if you want an image to print at a smaller size, you can enter new width and height values in the Image Size dialog box, shown in Exhibit 6-1. Under Pixel Dimensions, you can specify a new width and height in pixels or as a percentage. Under Document Size, you can specify a width and height in units such as inches or centimeters. This is useful for setting an image's size based on a specific target size, such as a fixed advertising space in a magazine.

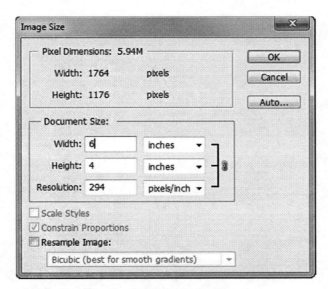

Exhibit 6-1: The Image Size dialog box

When you resize an image, you can specify whether to change the total number of pixels in the image (its pixel dimensions). If you check Resample Image, the image's resolution will stay constant as you change the width and height.

Increasing or decreasing the width or height while keeping the resolution constant forces Photoshop to add or remove pixels while trying to retain the original appearance of the image. This process, called *resampling*, can result in some blurring, called a *resampling error*, because Photoshop has to calculate the colors of the resulting pixels. The blurring is usually fairly slight, but it's best to avoid resampling when you can. In particular, you should avoid repeatedly resampling an image because each time you resample, the image will get a bit blurrier.

If you clear Resample Image, the image's pixel dimensions remain constant as you change the image's width and height. Therefore, the resolution is forced to change because the pixel dimensions can't.

If you want to increase an image's print size by a fairly small amount, you might be able to resize it without resampling and still maintain acceptable resolution. For example, if increasing the image size without resampling decreases its resolution from 300 ppi to 240 ppi, the image might still print better than if you were to resample the image, introducing some blurring due to resampling error.

Do it!

A-2: Resizing an image without resampling

Here's how	Here's why
1 Choose **Image, Image Size...**	To open the Image Size dialog box. Observe that this image is 48" × 32" but with a resolution of only 72 ppi.
2 Clear **Resample Image**	To specify that reducing the size of the image won't change the pixel dimensions. This will force the image resolution to increase.
3 Under Document Size, edit the Width box to read **6**	

```
┌─ Pixel Dimensions: 22.8M ──────────────┐
│                                        │
│    Width:  3456        pixels          │
│                                        │
│    Height: 2304        pixels          │
│                                        │
└────────────────────────────────────────┘

┌─ Document Size: ───────────────────────┐
│                                        │
│    Width:  [6    ]  [Inches      ▼] ┐  │
│                                     │  │
│    Height: [4    ]  [Inches      ▼] ┤⸉ │
│                                     │  │
│   Resolution: [576]  [Pixels/Inch ▼]┘  │
│                                        │
│  ☑ Scale Styles                        │
│  ☑ Constrain Proportions               │
│  ☐ Resample Image:                     │
└────────────────────────────────────────┘
```

The Height value automatically changes to 4 because Constrain Proportions is checked. Because the pixel dimensions are unchanged, the resolution is forced to increase.

4 Click **OK**	To change the image size.
5 Observe the status bar	The file size has not changed. If you had resized the image by adding or removing pixels (resampling), the file size would have changed.
Click the document size box	To view the new image size of 6" × 4".
6 Update the image	

Resampling

Explanation

If an image's resolution is significantly higher than necessary, you should reduce the resolution. For example, a digital-camera image that you want to post on the Web is likely to have a much higher resolution than necessary.

Reduce the resolution by checking Resample Image in the Image Size dialog box and setting either of the following:

- The pixel dimensions (as you would for the Web)
- The Width, Height, and Resolution (for, say, resizing a digital-camera image for printing when you don't want to transfer all of the extra file size unnecessarily)

If an image's resolution is somewhat lower than desired, you can check Resample Image and resize up. The result won't be as crisp as if the original had a high enough resolution to begin with, but you might improve the image enough to make it usable. Whenever possible, however, obtaining a new, original image at the resolution you need is preferable to resampling up in Photoshop.

Do it!

A-3:   Resampling an image

Here's how	Here's why
1 Save the image as **marketflyer**	(In the current topic folder.) You will eventually need to put this image on a Web page, so you'll need a separate copy for that purpose.
2 Choose **Image, Image Size...**	To open the Image Size dialog box.
Check **Resample Image**	To edit the image's pixel dimensions.
Under Pixel Dimensions, edit the Width box to read **600**	To set both the width and the height.
3 Observe the file size data at the top of the Image Size dialog box	Pixel Dimensions: 703.1K (was 22.8M) — Width: 600 Pixels Height: 400 Pixels
	The file size has been reduced considerably.
4 Click **OK**	To resample the image.
5 Choose **View, Actual Pixels**	To preview the image size as it will appear in a Web browser.
6 Update and close the image	

Topic B: Image canvas size

Explanation

The Photoshop *canvas* is all the available space used by an image. You can increase the canvas size to add more pixels around an image. You can also reduce the canvas size by *cropping* to remove part of an image.

The Crop tool

One way to increase or decrease the canvas size is to use the Crop tool. Although you can use the Crop tool to increase or decrease the canvas size, this tool is most typically used to decrease the canvas size by cutting away part of an image that you don't want.

Before you begin cropping an image, you might want to display the Info panel. The Info panel will display the width, height, and angle of the cropping marquee; this is useful when you want to crop to specific dimensions or to a specific angle.

To use the Crop tool to crop an image:

1 Select the Crop tool to enable the cropping marquee. All material outside the cropping marquee will be removed, unless you clear Delete Cropped Pixels on the options bar.

2 Adjust the cropping marquee so that it will crop the material you want, as follows:

- To resize the cropping area, drag the cropping marquee's handles.
- To move the cropping marquee to a different area of the image, drag from within it.
- To rotate the cropping marquee, drag from outside it. (Rotating a cropping marquee is useful for adjusting an image's rotation, but it can introduce some resampling errors.)

3 Press Enter to complete the crop.

The cropping marquee snaps to the edge of an image, and this behavior can be annoying if you're trying to crop out part of the image that is close to an edge. To prevent this, press Ctrl and drag to resize the marquee.

If you want to remove a cropping marquee without cropping the image, you can press Esc. If you want to crop an image to increase the canvas size, you can drag the cropping marquee handles beyond the image borders.

The rule of thirds

When professional photographers look through the viewfinder of their cameras, they often imagine the scene divided into a grid, much like a tic-tac-toe board. They try to place important compositional elements along the lines of the grid or at the intersections of these lines, as shown in Exhibit 6-2. This principle is called the *rule of thirds*.

When you crop an image in Photoshop, you can display a rule-of-thirds grid to help you decide which areas of the image to keep and which to discard. To do so, select the Crop tool; then, on the options bar, select Rule of Thirds from the View list. You can also select several other options.

Exhibit 6-2: Cropping with the Rule of Thirds grid

Do it!

B-1:   Cropping an image

The files for this activity are in Student Data folder **Unit 6\Topic B**.

Here's how	Here's why
1 Open Mixed fruit 1	
Save the image in Photoshop format as **My mixed fruit 1**	You'll crop and straighten the image.
2 In the Tools panel, click 	(The Crop tool.) A crop marquee appears around the image.

3 Using the resize handles, adjust the crop area as shown

The line created by the crates is slightly askew. You'll straighten it.

4 On the options bar, click

Drag down along the right side of the crate

To straighten the image relative to the line. When cropping an image, look for straight lines in the image for a reference.

5 Drag the marquee handles as shown

6 On the options bar, clear **Delete Cropped Pixels**	You want to retain the image pixels outside of the crop marquee in case you want to modify the crop later.
7 Press (↵ ENTER)	To crop and image.
8 Drag the top handle up	To see that the original image pixels are still available. (You may need to click the Crop tool again.)
Press (ESC)	
9 Update and close the image	

The Canvas Size dialog box

Explanation   Another way to increase or decrease the canvas size is to use the Canvas Size dialog box. For example, if you want to combine two images that are 100 × 100 pixels into a single file in which both images appear side by side, you can use the Canvas Size dialog box to double the width of one of the images so that it's 200 × 100 pixels. The canvas size will then be large enough to fit the second image, which you can drag to the other image as a new layer.

To use the Canvas Size dialog box to change an image's canvas size:

1 Set the background color to the color you want the added pixels to use.

2 Choose Image, Canvas Size to open the Canvas Size dialog box.

3 Under Anchor, click a square on the grid to specify the direction in which the canvas size will expand.

4 Edit the Width and Height boxes to specify the new values you want to use.

5 From the Canvas extension color list, specify the color you want the extended canvas to use. By default, it will use the current background color.

6 Click OK.

Do it!

B-2: Changing the canvas size

The files for this activity are in Student Data folder **Unit 6\Topic B**.

Here's how	Here's why
1 Open Apples 5	
Save the image as **My apples 5**	(In the current topic folder.) You'll increase the canvas size to add room at the top of the image.
2 Select the Eyedropper tool	You'll set the background color to green so the added pixels will match the existing green background.
Sample the green image background to set the background color	Press Alt as you click with the Eyedropper tool.
3 Choose **Image, Canvas Size...**	To open the Canvas Size dialog box.
Click the indicated anchor square	
	To specify where the additional pixels will appear.
4 Edit the Height box to read **12**	To increase the canvas size to 12".
Click **OK**	To add to the canvas size. The pixels added to the image to expand the canvas are green because that's the current background color.
5 Press (CTRL) + (0)	(If necessary.) To display the entire image.
6 Update and close the image	

Unit summary: Resizing images

Topic A   In this topic, you determined an image's **dimensions** and **resolution**. You also resized images with and without resampling.

Topic B   In this topic, you used the Crop tool and the Canvas Size dialog box to change an image's **canvas size**.

Independent practice activity

In this activity, you'll resize images with and without resampling. You'll also crop the image.

The files for this activity are in Student Data folder **Unit 6\Unit summary**.

1 Open Zoo flyer practice, and save the image in Photoshop format as **My zoo flyer practice**.

2 Resize the image to 6" wide without resampling.

3 Crop the image so that the words "Pangaea Zoo" fit the entire width of the image.

4 Change the image width to 600 pixels, with resampling. Update and close the image.

Review questions

1 In the Image Size dialog box, you increase an image's resolution from 72 to 120 with Resample Image checked. How does this change affect the image? [Choose all that apply.]

A The image's file size increases.

B The image will appear larger when printed.

C The image will appear smaller when printed.

D The image will appear larger if displayed in a Web browser.

2 In the Image Size dialog box, you increase an image's resolution from 72 to 120 with Resample Image cleared. How does this change affect your image?

A The image's file size increases.

B The image will appear larger when printed.

C The image will appear smaller when printed.

D The image will appear larger if displayed in a Web browser.

3 A good target resolution for color images you intend to print is:

A 1200 ppi

B 96 ppi

C 300 ppi

D The printer's resolution

4 When pixels are large enough that viewers can see stair-stepped, jagged edges, the image is _____.

5 True or false? It's important to set images intended for the Web to 96 ppi.

6 True or false? Resampling changes the number of pixels in an image while attempting to retain its basic appearance.

7 If you want to rotate an image while reducing its canvas size, you should use the _____ tool.

8 True or false? You can only reduce, not increase, the canvas size of an image by using the Canvas Size dialog box.

Unit 7

Managing files with Adobe Bridge

Complete this unit, and you'll know how to:

A Import files, navigate your computer's folder structure, and review files in Bridge.

B View and modify file metadata, and use metadata to find and filter files.

C Organize files by creating collections and smart collections.

D Output files by creating PDF contact sheets and Web galleries.

Topic A: Browsing files in Adobe Bridge

This topic covers the following ACE exam objectives for Photoshop CS6.

#	Objective
1.1	**Navigating between Adobe Bridge and your computer**
1.1.1	Navigating the computer structure using the path bar
1.1.2	Copying and pasting media in Bridge
1.1.3	Browsing subfolder structures
1.1.5	Using Review Mode
1.1.6	Importing images from a camera

Adobe Bridge and Mini Bridge

Explanation

If you use other applications in the Adobe Creative Suite, then you'll likely reuse images you create in Photoshop in other programs, such as InDesign and Illustrator. To manage files used in various CS6 applications, you can use Adobe Bridge. In addition, you can browse and manage images from within Photoshop by means of the Mini Bridge panel. Adobe Bridge and Mini Bridge communicate with one another to keep your assets up to date.

Download photos with Bridge

To transfer photos from your camera or memory card, use Adobe Bridge Photo Downloader in Adobe Bridge. Photo Downloader helps you organize photos by automating the process of saving and renaming files, creating subfolders based on the photo dates, converting files to another format, and saving copies. You can also use templates to apply metadata.

To download photos:

1 Connect your camera or memory card to the computer.

2 In Adobe Bridge, start Photo Downloader in either of the following ways:

- Choose File, Get Photos from Camera.
- Click the Get Photos from Camera button on the application bar.

You can also choose Download images in the Windows AutoPlay dialog box, which appears when you connect a camera to your computer.

3 Select the source of the photos from the list. The source can be the camera—if it is connected to the computer—or a card reader.

4 Specify a location where the pictures will be stored.

5 Choose the method by which subfolders will be created: subfolders by shot date in various formats; the date of import; a custom name; or no subfolders.

6 Choose a method by which the files are renamed—new names by shot date in various formats, the date of import, a custom name, or shot date plus a custom name—or choose to not rename files.

7　Choose among several additional operations:

- Open Adobe Bridge — If you start Photo Downloader from within Windows AutoPlay, Bridge will start after the photos are imported.

- Convert To DNG — This option converts the camera's proprietary RAW photos to DNG, a common archive format that can be read by many applications. Click Settings to choose various options.

- Delete Original Files — This option clears the source files from the camera or card.

- Save Copies to — You can choose a location for storing copies of the original files.

8　Click Get Media.

In addition to these options, the Advanced Dialog offers choices of metadata you can apply to the files. You can choose a template and apply creator and copyright values. The Advanced Dialog also displays thumbnails of the images. By using the thumbnails, you can deselect an image so it isn't imported. The Advanced Dialog of the Photo Downloader is shown in Exhibit 7-1.

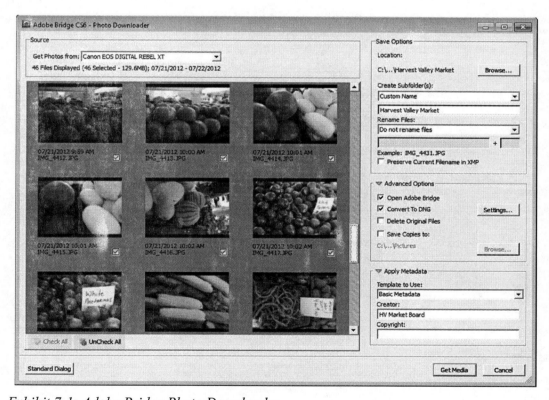

Exhibit 7-1: Adobe Bridge Photo Downloader

Do it!

A-1: Importing images in Bridge

Here's how	Here's why
1 Click  ⊞	
Click **All Programs**	
Choose **Adobe Bridge CS6**	To start Adobe Bridge.
2 At the top of the window, click  ⊡	(Under the menu bar.) To start Photo Downloader.
3 Under Source, display the **Get Photos from** list	The name of a connected camera or card reader will appear here. If you connect the camera after starting Downloader, choose <Refresh List> to rescan the system to find a device.
4 Under Import Settings, click **Browse…**	
Navigate to the current topic folder and select **Harvest Valley Market**	This will be the main folder to which your photos will be imported.
Click **Select Folder**	
5 Check **Convert To DNG**	To convert the camera's RAW photo files to the more widely used DNG format.
Click **Settings…**	To open the DNG Conversion Settings dialog box.
6 From the JPEG Preview list, select **Full Size**	Creating JPEGs is a good idea when you want to display the photos in an application that doesn't support RAW or DNG files.
7 Observe the settings under Image Conversion Method	The paragraph discusses the advantages of preserving the RAW image data.
8 Observe the settings under Original Raw File	The paragraph discusses the advantage of embedding the RAW image file.
Click **OK**	
9 Click **Advanced Dialog**	(At the bottom-left.) To expand the dialog box to show more options.
10 In the Creator box, type **HV Market Board**	(In the Apply Metadata section.) To add this metadata to the imported files.
11 Click **Cancel**	To close Photo Downloader without importing photos.

Adobe Bridge file navigation

Explanation

Files managed with Bridge don't need to be stored in a single location on your computer. Consequently, it can be challenging to know the locations of the various files you're working with. Fortunately, there are several ways to navigate your computer's file structure when using Bridge.

To navigate files with Adobe Bridge:

1 Launch Bridge.

2 Click the Folders tab.

3 Navigate to the desired file folder by using the tree view. Click a folder to select it. Any content that Bridge can manage will be displayed in the Content panel.

4 Select a workspace option. A few options are displayed on the application bar, as shown in Exhibit 7-2; others are accessed through the Workspace menu. You can access the same options from the Window menu.

5 If you want to enlarge or shrink the thumbnails, drag the Thumbnail slider.

6 In Essentials view, click a thumbnail to display a preview and *metadata* (additional information about the file, such as its kind, modification date, dimensions, and resolution).

7 Click a view button to select display options.

8 To open a file, either double-click its thumbnail to open it in the default Adobe Creative Suite application for that file type; or right-click it, choose Open With, and choose an application.

Path bar   Workspace menu

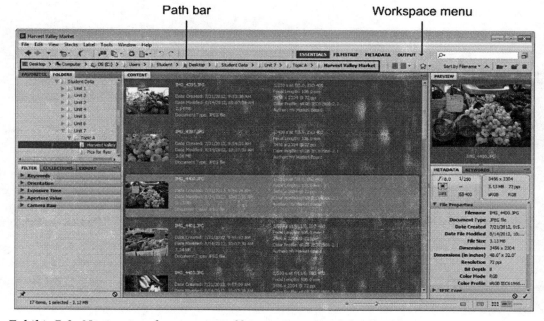

Exhibit 7-2: Navigating the computer file structure in Adobe Bridge

The path bar

When navigating in Bridge, the path bar shows the location of the currently selected folder. You can also use the path bar to navigate. To do so:

- Click in the path bar to go to that location.
- Right-click an item in the path bar to show other folders at the same root level; then click to navigate to them.
- Drag an item from the Content panel to the path bar to go to that item's location.
- Enter a path manually by clicking the last item in the path bar; when finished, press Enter to go to that location.

Mini Bridge

You can manage assets that you want to share between Creative Suite applications from within Photoshop by using *Mini Bridge*, shown in Exhibit 7-3. Mini Bridge is a panel that appears, minimized at the bottom of the application frame, in the default Essentials workspace. When you open the Mini Bridge panel, you'll see the Navigation pod and the Content pod. Use the Navigation pod to find the files you want to manage, which will be shown in the Content pod. As with Adobe Bridge, Mini Bridge has buttons you can use to navigate and to change the view of the selected files.

Exhibit 7-3: The Mini Bridge panel in Photoshop

Copying and pasting media

You can use Bridge to change the location of files and folders on your computer. You might, for example, want to copy a few images from one folder into a folder in another location. To copy an image or folder, select it and choose Edit, Copy (or press Ctrl+C). Then navigate to the new location and choose Edit, Paste (or press Ctrl+V).

If you want to copy files or folders to another location without navigating to that location, right-click the selection and, from the shortcut menu, choose Copy to display a submenu of locations you can select. If the location you want isn't shown, choose Choose Folder.

Do it!

A-2: Navigating files in Adobe Bridge and Mini Bridge

The files for this activity are in Student Data folder **Unit 7\Topic A**.

Here's how	Here's why
1 Click the **Folders** tab	(The Folders tab is next to the Favorites tab, under the path bar.) To show the tree view of your computer's contents.
Navigate to the current topic folder	
Select the **Harvest Valley Market** folder	To display thumbnails for the files in this folder.
2 In the bottom-right corner of the Bridge window, click ▬ ≣	(The View content as details button.) To change the display in the Content panel to show information about each image.
3 Drag the Thumbnail slider to the left	To reduce the size of the image thumbnails.
4 Select **IMG_4400.JPG**	(The third image.) You'll copy it and paste it to another location.
Press (CTRL) + (C)	To copy the image.
5 Observe the path bar	It shows the location of the files on your computer.
Right-click the path bar as shown	To show other folders in this location.
Choose **Pics for flyer**	To go to that location.
6 Press (CTRL) + (V)	To paste the image you copied. The image now appears in both folders.
7 In the path bar, click the current unit topic	
Double-click **Harvest Valley Market**	In the Content panel.
8 Double-click **IMG_4395.JPG**	To open it in Photoshop.

9	Click the **Mini Bridge** panel tab	Mini Bridge Timeline
		(At the bottom of the application frame.) To open the Mini Bridge panel.
10	In the Navigation pod, navigate to the current topic folder	
	Select the **Harvest Valley Market** folder	To display thumbnails in the Contenr pod.
11	Double-click **IMG_4397.JPG**	To open it in Photoshop in a new tab.
12	Close both images	Press Ctrl+W twice.
13	Double-click the Mini Bridge panel tab	To collapse it.
	Close Photoshop	

Preview files in Adobe Bridge

Explanation

When using Bridge, you can preview files without opening them in their applications. There are several methods to do so.

The Preview panel

When you select a file, Bridge automatically displays a preview of it in the Preview panel (if the Preview panel is open). You can drag the edges of the Preview panel to make it as large or small as you'd like. In addition, when you click in the Preview panel, the cursor becomes a *loupe* that you can use to magnify areas of the preview, as shown in Exhibit 7-4. You can use the + and - keys to zoom in and out while using the loupe. To close the loupe, click inside of it.

Exhibit 7-4: Using the loupe in the Preview panel

One-click preview

With a file selected, press Spacebar to display the file in full-screen mode. When in full-screen mode, click the file to enlarge it to 100%, and click again to zoom back to full-screen view. Use the Left Arrow and Right Arrow keys to navigate to the next or previous photo. Click Spacebar again to return to Bridge.

Review Mode

You can view multiple files at once by using Review Mode. To do so, select the files you want to review and, on the application bar, click the Refine button and choose Review Mode. (You can also choose View, Review Mode or press Ctrl+B.)

Review Mode displays the selected files in a carousel view. You can use the Left Arrow and Right Arrow keys to navigate to the next or previous photo. Additionally, press the Down Arrow key to remove the foremost file from Review Mode, and press Up Arrow to add it back. Like the Preview panel, Review Mode also has a loupe. To use it, click in the image to activate it, and then drag to position it. To close it, click inside the loupe area.

To exit Review Mode, click the close button at the bottom-right or press Esc.

Exhibit 7-5: Review Mode

Do it!

A-3: Using Review Mode

Here's how	Here's why
1 On the application bar, click ⬚▾	(The Refine button.) To display a menu.
Choose **Review Mode**	To display the files in the current folder in Review Mode.
2 Press (→) twice	To scroll through the images.
3 Press (↓)	To remove one of the images of the onions from Review Mode.
Press (↓) twice	To remove the image of the peaches and of the squash.
4 Remove one of the images of the apples	Scroll with the Right Arrow and Left Arrow keys to select it, then press Down Arrow.
5 Remove one of the images of the tomatoes	
6 Remove eight more images	When you only have four images displayed, Review Mode changes to show all four at once.
7 Click one of the images	The cursor changes to a loupe.
Drag the loupe over the image	
Click in the loupe	To close it.
8 Press (ESC)	To exit Review Mode.

Topic B: Working with metadata

This topic covers the following ACE exam objectives for Photoshop CS6.

#	Objective
1.1	**Navigating between Adobe Bridge and your computer**
1.1.4	Working with filters
1.2	**Working with metadata**
1.2.1	Viewing, modifying, and replacing metadata in images
1.2.2	Viewing, modifying, and replacing metadata in graphics
1.2.3	Viewing, modifying, and replacing metadata in video

Metadata

Explanation

If you plan to share an image with others, or you expect that you'll need to retrieve it later from among many images, it's helpful to add *metadata*, or additional information about the image, such as keywords and author names. Files generated by digital cameras usually already have some metadata pertaining to camera settings. This information is stored along with the image data. You or others can then use applications such as Adobe Bridge or other image catalog programs to view and search by the metadata.

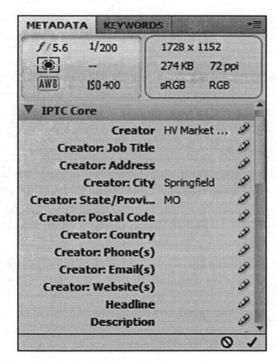

Exhibit 7-6: The Metadata panel

Metadata and keywords in Adobe Bridge

To view metadata for a file, select it and click the Metadata tab. You can also choose File, File Info to open a dialog box that contains metadata. Additionally, two of the views in Bridge display metadata in the Content pane—from the View menu, choose As List or As Details.

You can use Adobe Bridge to add metadata to multiple files at once. To add metadata in Bridge, select one or more files, and choose File, File Info to open a dialog box. You can also enter data directly on the Metadata tab or the Keywords tab. Metadata that you can edit on the Metadata tab has a pencil icon next to it, as shown in Exhibit 7-6. To edit the metadata, click the pencil icon and edit the field; when finished, click the Apply button or, to discard the changes, click the Cancel button.

If you use different types of files—images, graphics, videos—you'll notice that the kind of metadata displayed for each one is slightly different. For example, when viewing the metadata for an Adobe Illustrator graphic, you'll see categories for fonts, plates, and document swatches that don't appear when you're viewing the metadata for an image.

Metadata templates and importing metadata

Bridge uses the XMP (Extended Metadata Platform) to store metadata. You can take advantage of this to save metadata templates to use with other XMP-enable applications—such as Adobe InDesign—or to import templates created in other applications. To create a template, choose Tools, Create Metadata Template. To import a template, the template should be stored in the Metadata Templates folder. (To locate this folder, choose Tools, Create Metadata Template; in the dialog box, display the pop-up menu and choose Show Templates Folder.) Choose Tools, Append Metadata or Tools, Replace Metadata to view the available templates—appending metadata affects only fields that are not currently populated, while replacing it replaces any existing metadata with metadata from the template.

You can also import metadata, which gives you more control over how the metadata is handled. To do so:

1　Choose File, File Info.

2　From the pop-up menu at the bottom of the dialog box, choose Import.

3　Select an import option:

- **Clear existing properties and replace with template properties** – Replaces all existing metadata with metadata from the template.

- **Keep original metadata, but replace matching properties from template** – When properties differ, replaces those properties with metadata from the template.

- **Keep original metadata, but append matching properties from template** – Only adds metadata from the template if that property currently is empty.

4　Click OK to select the template.

Keywords

By default, Adobe Bridge contains three keyword sets: Events, People, and Places. To edit a keyword, right-click it and choose Rename from the shortcut menu. To create a new keyword, right-click anywhere in the set and choose New Keyword.

You also can create new keywords by clicking the New Keyword and New Sub Keyword buttons at the bottom of the Keywords tab. When you click the New Keyword button, a keyword is created in a set named Other Keywords; enter a name to save the new keyword. You can drag keywords to move them to any existing set.

Keywords appear in italics if you imported them as metadata from another program, added them via the File Info dialog box, or added them by clicking the New Keyword button. To make these keywords permanent, right-click them and choose Make Persistent. Persistent keywords will always be available for you to apply to other files in Bridge.

Do it!

B-1: Viewing and modifying metadata

The files for this activity are in Student Data folder **Unit 7\Topic B**.

Here's how	Here's why
1 In Adobe Bridge, navigate to the current topic folder	Use the Folders tab or the path bar.
2 Select **IMG_4395.JPG**	
3 Choose **File, File Info...**	To open the dialog box for entering metadata.
Observe the Author box	The Author metadata was added when the images were imported with Bridge.
In the Keywords box, enter **market, beets**	
Click **OK**	To close the dialog box and add the metadata to the file.
4 Press CTRL + A	You'll apply metadata to all of the images.
5 Click the **Metadata** panel	(If necessary.) To display the file's metadata.
Click as shown	Color Profile sRGB IEC61966... ▶ IPTC Core ▶ IPTC Extension
	To expand the list. The information you entered appears in the Creator and Keywords boxes.
6 Next to Creator: City, click 🖉	To activate the metadata field.
Type **Springfield**	
7 Press TAB	To go to the next field.
Type **MO**	

8	At the bottom of the panel, click ☑	(The Apply button.) To apply the changes.
9	Click the **Keywords** panel	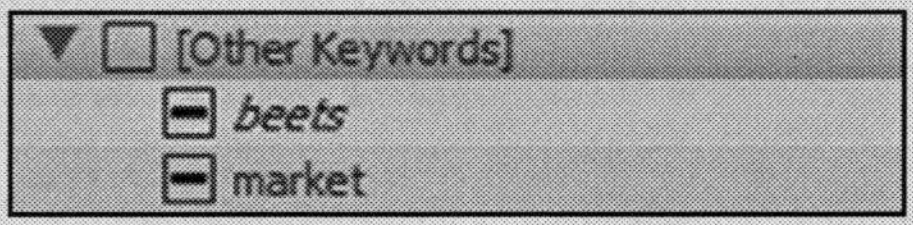 ▼ ☐ [Other Keywords] ⊟ *beets* ⊟ market In the Other Keywords set, the keywords you added are shown, indicating that they're applied to some—but not all—of the selected images.
	Check **market**	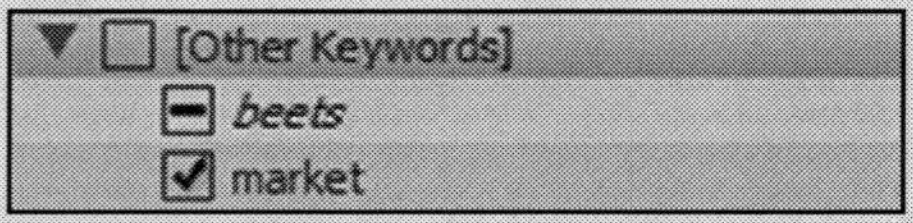 ▼ ☐ [Other Keywords] ⊟ *beets* ☑ market To apply the keyword to all of the images.
10	Press ⌜CTRL⌝ and click the following images: **IMG_4401.JPG** **IMG_4406.JPG** **IMG_4416.JPG** **IMG_4417.JPG** **IMG_4424.JPG**	To deselect them.
11	In the keyword list, select **[Other Keywords]** Click 🗒	(The New Sub Keyword button is at the bottom of the Keywords panel.) To add a new keyword in the Other Keywords set.
	Type **veggies** and press ⌜↵ ENTER⌝ Check **veggies**	▼ ☐ [Other Keywords] ⊟ *beets* ☑ market ☑ veggies To add the keyword to the selected images.
12	In the Keywords panel, right-click **market**	You work with pictures of the market frequently, so you'll make this keyword persistent so it always appears in Adobe Bridge.
	Choose **Make Persistent**	The word is no longer italicized; this indicates that it will remain in Bridge even after the program is closed and re-opened.
13	Press ⌜CTRL⌝ + ⌜SHIFT⌝ + ⌜A⌝	To deselect all of the images.

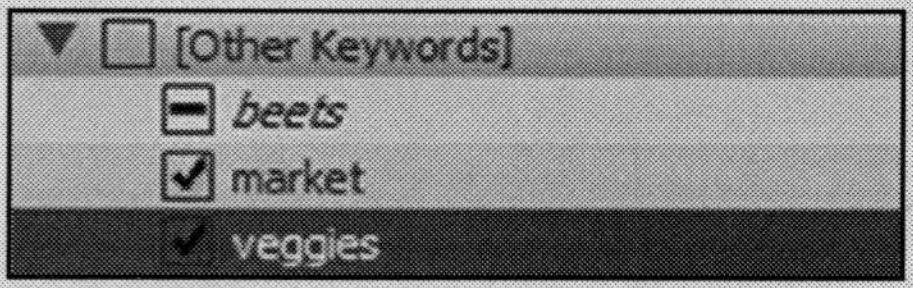

Finding files by using metadata

Explanation

You can search for files that have common metadata and keywords by using Bridge. Dates, subjects, names, and locations are examples of common search terms, though any number of possible criteria could be used. This is a very valuable capability when managing a vast number of images in a collection.

To search metadata, enter a term in the search bar at the right of the application bar and press Enter. To clear a search, click the Cancel button at the top-right of the Content panel.

You can also choose Edit, Find (or press Ctrl+F) to open the Find dialog box, shown in Exhibit 7-7, which gives you more control over searching.

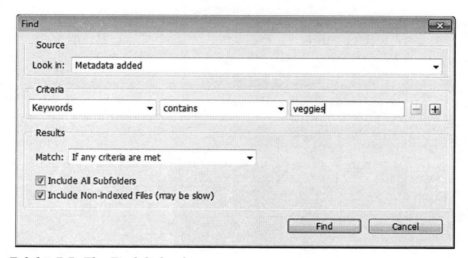

Exhibit 7-7: The Find dialog box

The Filter panel

For even greater control when searching files, you can use the Filter panel. This method has the advantage of being able to modify a search "on the fly." The Filter panel, shown in Exhibit 7-8, displays the metadata associated with the files in the Content panel. Expand the headings and select the desired metadata to display the associated files. If you want to preserve the filter criteria when switching to other folders, click the pin icon at the bottom-left of the panel.

To specify which metadata is shown in the Filter panel, display the panel menu and select or deselect the desired options. (By default, all of the options are selected.)

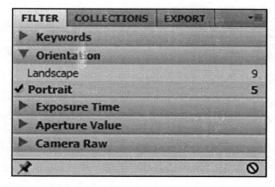

Exhibit 7-8: The Filter panel

Do it!   **B-2:   Finding and filtering images in Bridge**

Here's how	Here's why
1 Press CTRL + F	To open the Find dialog box. You'll search for images containing a common keyword.
2 Under criteria, from the first list, select **Keywords**	
From the second list, select **contains**	If necessary.
In the third box, type **veggies**	
Click **Find**	To display only the images with the veggies keyword.
3 In the Filter panel, click **Orientation**	You're looking for images that will fit a particular spot in a newsletter.
Click **Portrait**	
4 In the Content panel, click ⊗	(The Cancel button.) To show all the images.

Topic C: Organizing collections

This topic covers the following ACE exam objectives for Photoshop CS6.

#	Objective
1.3	**Organizing collections**
1.3.1	Creating collections
1.3.2	Creating Smart collections
1.3.3	Creating Favorites for groups of images and media

Collections and Favorites

Explanation

When you import or view folders of files in Bridge, it's likely those folders will contain a mixture of file types. For example, if you import images from a camera, you might have several pictures from one event, one picture from another, and so on. Using Bridge, you can create collections and Favorites to more easily associate your files and more quickly find important ones.

Collections

Collections are essentially folders of files that exist only in Bridge. They're a way for you to associate files as you'd like, rather than by their location on your computer.

To create a new, empty collection, click the Collections tab and then click the New Collection button, shown in Exhibit 7-9. Type a name and press Enter. To edit the name of an existing collection, click its name on the Collections tab and type.

Once a collection exists, simply drag files from the Content tab to the collection folder (or copy and paste them) to add them.

Alternatively, you can select files first and then click the New Collection button—when you do, a new collection will be created with the selected files.

To delete a collection, select it and click the Delete Collection button in the Collections panel.

Exhibit 7-9: The Collections panel

Smart collections

You can automatically add files to a collection by using smart collections. Smart collections continuously look in the specified location for files containing metadata matching the criteria you tell them to look for. When a file is found, Bridge adds it to the smart collection, even if it's a new file.

To create a smart collection:

1   Click the New Smart collection button on the Collections panel.
2   In the Smart Collection dialog box, from the Look in list, select the location you want Bridge to look and monitor for files.
3   Under Criteria, from the leftmost list, select the metadata you want to search for.
4   From the middle list, select an option to constrain the search.
5   From the rightmost list, either enter or select (based on the criteria) the search term.
6   To add more criteria, click the plus-sign icon.
7   Under Results, from the Match list, select whether you want to match any or all of the criteria.
8   Check Include All Subfolders if you want Bridge to search all subfolders of the selected Source location.
9   Click Save.

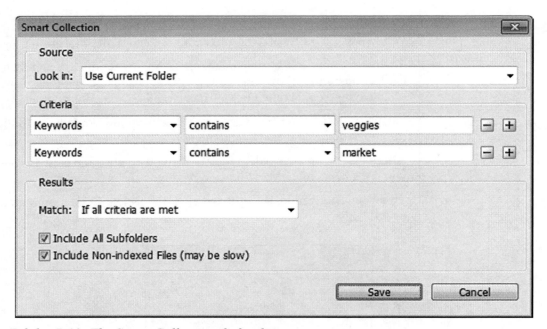

Exhibit 7-10: The Smart Collection dialog box

Favorites

The Favorites tab shows, by default, some commonly used folders and locations, such as the desktop and your documents folder. You can also add folders to the Favorites tab so that you can navigate to them more quickly. To do so, drag a folder from the Content panel to the Favorites panel.

Do it!

C-1: Creating collections

The files for this activity are in Student Data folder **Unit 7\Topic C**.

Here's how	Here's why
1 Navigate to the current topic folder	
2 Select **IMG_4397.JPG**	You'll select some images for possible use in the market newsletter.
Press ⌈CTRL⌋ and select **IMG_4401.JPG** and **IMG_4406.JPG**	
3 Click the **Collections** tab	
4 Click [icon]	(The New Collection button is at the bottom of the Collections panel.) A message box appears, asking if you want to include the selected files.
Click **Yes**	To create a new collection containing the selected images. The collection's name is active.
Type **Newsletter pics** and press ⌈↵ ENTER⌋	Next, you'll create a smart collection to automatically display files with specific criteria.
5 Navigate to the current topic folder	
6 Click [icon]	(The New Smart Collection button.) To open the Smart Collection dialog box.
7 From the Look in list, select **Use Current Folder**	
8 Under Criteria, from the leftmost list, select **Keywords**	If necessary.
From the middle list, select **Contains**	If necessary.
In the box, type **veggies**	

9 Click ⊞   To add another set of criteria.

Specify the indicated criteria

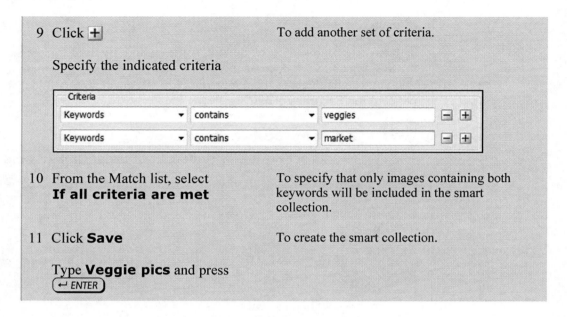

10 From the Match list, select   To specify that only images containing both
    If all criteria are met   keywords will be included in the smart
                                             collection.

11 Click **Save**   To create the smart collection.

Type **Veggie pics** and press
⏎ ENTER

Topic D: Outputting projects

This topic covers the following ACE exam objectives for Photoshop CS6.

#	Objective
1.4	**Outputting projects to PDF and for the Web**
1.4.1	Creating PDF documents and PDF slide shows
1.4.2	Creating HTML and Flash-based Websites
1.4.3	Uploading a Website to a hosting provider by using FTP

PDF documents and websites

Explanation

There are several ways you can output files in Bridge. For example, you can create a PDF document or a website. You can also customize a PDF to automatically display a slideshow.

Contact sheets and slideshows

When you're working with multiple photos, it's sometimes helpful to print them so that you can see them all at once. For example, you might have multiple exposures of a single scene, and you want to choose the best one for editing. You can print them together by creating a PDF contact sheet.

To create a contact sheet:

1 In Bridge, select the images you want to include in the contact sheet.
2 Choose Window, Workspace, Output.
3 At the top of the Output panel, click PDF to show the PDF options.
4 From the Template list, select one of the contact sheet options.
5 Customize the PDF as desired by specifying settings in the Document, Layout, Overlays, Header, Footer, Playback, and Watermark sections.
6 Click Save.

PDF slideshows

You can customize a PDF document to display a slideshow. To do so, in the PDF section of the Output panel, scroll down to the Playback heading, shown in Exhibit 7-11, and select the desired options.

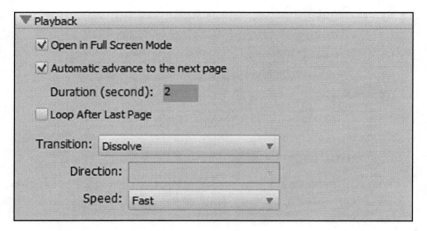

Exhibit 7-11: PDF slideshow options

Do it!

D-1:   Creating a contact sheet

The files for this activity are in Student Data folder **Unit 7\Topic D**.

Here's how	Here's why
1 Navigate to the current topic folder	
Press CTRL + A	To select all of the images.
Press CTRL and click the **Web gallery** folder	To deselect it.
2 On the application bar, click ▢➔▾ and choose **Output to Web or PDF**	To activate the Output workspace.
3 In the Output panel, click **PDF**	If necessary.
4 From the Template list, select **4*5 Contact Sheet**	You'll start with the template but modify the settings.
Under Document, from the Page Preset list, select **U.S. Paper**	To set the Size to Letter.
Under Layout, edit the Columns box to read **2**	

5 At the top of the Output panel, click **Refresh Preview**

After a few moments, a preview of the contact sheet appears in the Output Preview window.

6 Scroll to the heading Playback

Check **Open in Full Screen Mode**

Check **Automatic advance to the next page**

Edit the Duration box to read **2**

From the Transition list, select **Dissolve**

7 At the bottom of the panel, check **View PDF After Save**

8 Click **Save**

To open the Save dialog box.

Navigate to the current topic folder

In the File name box, enter **My contact sheet**

Click **Save**

After a few moments, the contact sheet opens in Adobe Reader and a warning box appears.

Click **Yes**

To begin the slideshow.

9 Press (ESC)

To exit Full Screen Mode.

Close Adobe Reader

To return to Bridge.

Creating Web galleries

Explanation

A *Web gallery* is a website that has been designed primarily to display images. A Web gallery typically has a page containing image thumbnails that you can click to navigate to pages showing the full-size images.

You can use Adobe Bridge to generate the HTML code necessary to display your images as a web gallery. After generating the files, you can upload them to a website.

To generate a Web gallery:

1 In Bridge, navigate to the folder that contains the images you want to use.
2 Select the images you want to use.
3 On the application bar, click the Output button and select Output to Web or PDF.
4 In the Output pane, click Web Gallery.
5 From the Template list, select a template.
6 Modify the options in the Site Info and Color Palette sections as desired.
7 Click Preview in Browser. The images and generated HTML files are placed in the folder you specified.
8 In the Create Gallery section of the Output panel, select Save to Disk. Click Browse and select a location. Click Save.

Uploading a website by using FTP

Once you've created a web gallery, you need a way to get it online. If you have FTP access to a website, you can upload the gallery directly from Bridge. To do so, enter the server information in the Create Gallery section of the Output panel, as shown in Exhibit 7-12.

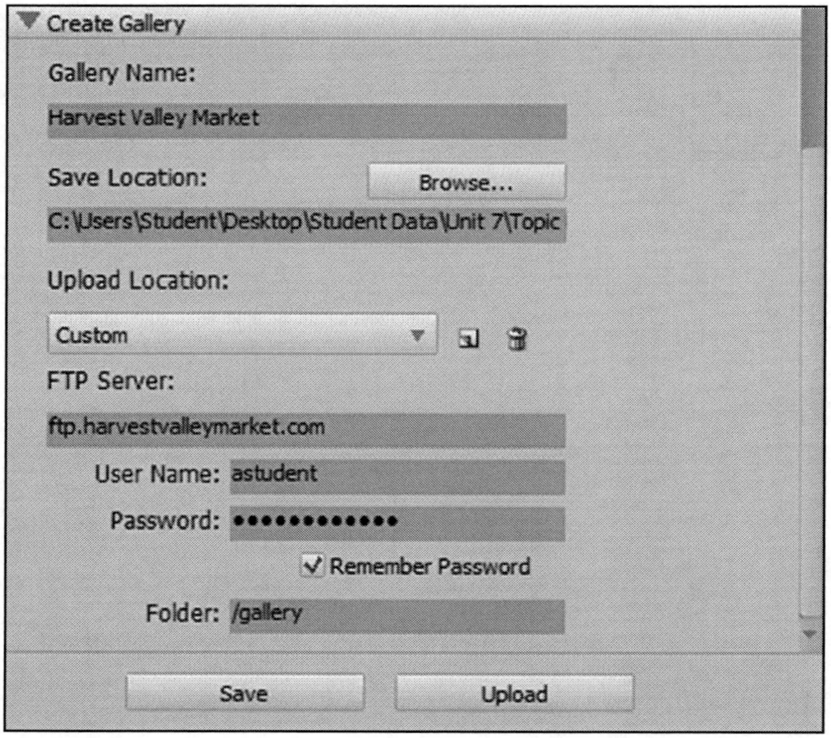

Exhibit 7-12: Create Gallery settings

Do it!   ## D-2:   Creating a Web gallery

The files for this activity are in Student Data folder **Unit 7\Topic D**.

Here's how	Here's why
1 At the top of the Output panel, click **Web Gallery**	
2 Press ⌐CTRL⌐ + ⌐A⌐	(If necessary.) To select all of the images in this folder.
3 From the Template list, select **Filmstrip**	
4 Under Site Info, edit the Gallery Title box to read **Harvest Valley Market**	
Edit the Gallery Caption box to read **Fresh from the farm**	
Edit the About This Gallery box to read **Here are some samples of what you'll find**	
In the Your Name box, enter your name	
In the E-mail Address box, enter **admin@harvestvalleymarket.com**	
5 In the Color Palette section, click the black color swatch next to Main	To open the Color dialog box.
Select a green color	
Click **OK**	
6 Click **Preview in Browser**	(At the top of the panel.) To preview the gallery.
Click one of the thumbnail images	To view a larger image.
Close the browser window	To return to Bridge.
7 Scroll to the bottom of the Output panel	To view the Create Gallery section.
Edit the Gallery Name box to read **Harvest Valley Market**	

8 Next to Save Location, click
   Browse

   Navigate to the **Web gallery**   You'll save the Web gallery files here.
   folder in the current topic folder

   Click **OK**

9 Observe the FTP Server fields   If you had this information, you could upload
                                            the gallery to a website.

10 At the bottom of the panel, click   After a few moments, the Create Gallery dialog
   Save   box appears.

   Click **OK**   To close the dialog box.

11 Close Adobe Bridge

12 In Windows Explorer, navigate to the
   Web gallery\Adobe Web Gallery\resources\images
   folder in the current topic folder

                                            To view the folders in the images folder. Images
                                            were saved in large, medium, and thumbnail
                                            formats.

Unit summary: Managing files with Adobe Bridge

Topic A   In this topic, you learned how to **import images** from a digital camera into Bridge. You also used Bridge to **navigate your computer's folder structure** to find files. And you used **Review Mode** to preview files.

Topic B   In this topic, you learned how to view **metadata** attached to files. You also added metadata by using the **File, File Info** command and the **Metadata panel**. You created keywords and added them to images by using the **Keywords panel**. Then you used metadata to **find** and **filter** files in Bridge.

Topic C   In this topic, you organized files in Bridge by creating **collections**. You also learned how to create **smart collections** to automatically add files to folders in Bridge.

Topic D   In this topic, you output files by creating a **PDF contact sheet** to show previews of images, and you learned how to specify slideshow settings for a PDF. You also created a **Web gallery**.

Independent practice activity

In this activity, you'll add metadata to images, create collections, and create a Web gallery.

The files for this activity are in Student Data folder **Unit 7\Unit summary**.

1 In the current topic folder, view the images in Bridge.

2 Add existing keywords or create new ones so that each image has at least one keyword associated with it.

3 Create a smart collection (or more than one) to organize the images in Bridge.

4 Create a Web gallery that uses only some of the images.

5 Close Bridge.

Review questions

1 True or false: You can add some metadata to images when importing them from a camera into Bridge.

2 Describe how you can use Bridge to copy files from one folder to another in a separate location on your computer.

3 You've selected several images in Bridge, and the Keywords panel displays the following. What does this mean?

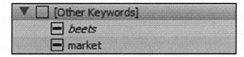

A These keywords shouldn't be used for the selected images.

B All of the images' metadata contain these keywords.

C None of the images' metadata contain these keywords.

D Some of the images' metadata contain these keywords.

4 You want to browse images according to different metadata criteria, but you're unsure which metadata you want to use. How can you do this?

5 True or false: Creating a collection in Bridge changes the locations of files on your computer.

6 You'll be continually downloading images to your computer and want to keep them organized automatically according to their metadata. What's the best way to do so?

A Create collections.

B Create smart collections.

C Create metadata filters.

D Use the path bar.

7 True or false: When creating a Web gallery, you could have Bridge upload the gallery to an FTP site, if you have the login information.

Appendix A

ACE exam objectives map

This appendix covers these additional topics:

A ACE exam objectives for Photoshop CS6, with references to corresponding coverage in ILT Series courseware.

Topic A: Comprehensive exam objectives

Explanation   The following table lists the Adobe Certified Expert (ACE) exam objectives for Photoshop CS6 and indicates where each objective is covered in conceptual explanations, hands-on activities, or both.

1.0 Managing assets using Adobe Bridge

#	Objective	Course level	Conceptual information	Supporting activities
1.1	**Navigating between Adobe Bridge and your computer**			
1.1.1	Navigating the computer structure using the path bar	Basic	Unit 7, Topic A	A-2
1.1.2	Copying and pasting media in Bridge	Basic	Unit 7, Topic A	A-2
1.1.3	Browsing subfolder structures	Basic	Unit 7, Topic A	A-2
1.1.4	Working with filters	Basic	Unit 7, Topic B	B-2
1.1.5	Using Review Mode	Basic	Unit 7, Topic A	A-3
1.1.6	Importing images from a camera	Basic	Unit 7, Topic A	A-1
1.2	**Working with metadata**			
1.2.1	Viewing, modifying, and replacing metadata in images	Basic	Unit 7, Topic B	B-1
1.2.2	Viewing, modifying, and replacing metadata in graphics	Basic	Unit 7, Topic B	B-1
1.2.3	Viewing, modifying, and replacing metadata in video	Basic	Unit 7, Topic B	B-1
1.3	**Organizing collections**			
1.3.1	Creating collections	Basic	Unit 7, Topic C	C-1
1.3.2	Creating Smart collections	Basic	Unit 7, Topic C	C-1
1.3.3	Creating Favorites for groups of images and media	Basic	Unit 7, Topic C	
1.4	**Outputting projects to PDF and for the Web**			
1.4.1	Creating PDF documents and PDF slide shows	Basic	Unit 7, Topic D	D-1
1.4.2	Creating HTML and Flash-based Websites	Basic	Unit 7, Topic D	D-2
1.4.3	Uploading a Website to a hosting provider by using FTP	Basic	Unit 7, Topic D	D-2
1.5	**Automating multiple images in Bridge**			
1.5.1	Using Batch Rename	Production	Unit 1, Topic D	D-6
1.5.2	Using the Photoshop Image Processor	Production	Unit 1, Topic D	D-1
1.5.3	Calling batch actions from within Photoshop	Production	Unit 1, Topic D	D-5
1.5.4	Using Merge to HDR Pro	Production	Unit 2, Topic B	
1.5.5	Differentiating between using Camera Raw in Bridge versus using Camera Raw and Photoshop	Production	Unit 1, Topic C	

2.0 Using Camera Raw

#	Objective	Course level	Conceptual information	Supporting activities
2.1	**Basic single image adjustment**			
2.1.1	Determining the correct white balance for an image	Production	Unit 1, Topic A	A-1
2.1.2	Adjusting exposure and contrast	Production	Unit 1, Topic A	A-2
2.1.3	Understanding the differences between clarity, vibrance, and saturation	Production	Unit 1, Topic A	A-3
2.1.4	Determining the benefits of Raw format and limitations of saving images as JPG	Production	Unit 1, Topic A	
2.2	**Selective image corrections**			
2.2.1	Successfully applying a local correction to an image and modifying the selection using Camera Raw tools	Production	Unit 1, Topic B	B-1
2.2.2	Using Targeted Adjustment tools	Production	Unit 1, Topic B	B-2
2.2.3	Using the Graduated Filter tool	Production	Unit 1, Topic B	B-3
2.3	**Batch processing and editing**			
2.3.1	Syncing develop settings in Camera Raw	Production	Unit 1, Topic C	C-3
2.3.2	Processing JPG images in Camera Raw and Photoshop	Production	Unit 1, Topic B	B-1
2.3.3	Defining edit presets	Production	Unit 1, Topic C	C-1
2.4	**Understanding Process Version and workflow options**			
2.4.1	Understanding the differences between Process Version 2010 and 2012	Production	Unit 1, Topic A	
2.4.2	Explaining the purpose of Process Version and how it applies to the development of images in Camera Raw	Production	Unit 1, Topic A	
2.5	**Automating multiple images**			
2.5.1	Development of presets and snapshots	Production	Unit 1, Topic C	C-1
2.5.2	Applying presets to single and multiple images	Production	Unit 1, Topic C	C-1
2.5.3	Exporting image settings to use in another computer	Production	Unit 1, Topic C	

3.0 Understanding Photoshop fundamentals

#	Objective	Course level	Conceptual information	Supporting activities
3.1	**Navigating the Photoshop workspace**			
3.1.1	Zooming and moving around an image in Photoshop	Basic	Unit 1, Topic B	B-3
3.1.2	Setting up guides, rulers, and grid units	Basic	Unit 1, Topic B	B-4
3.1.3	Using keyboard shortcuts to temporarily select tools	Basic	Unit 1, Topic B	B-3
3.1.4	Selecting, modifying, and replacing Photoshop workspace and keyboard shortcuts	Basic	Unit 1, Topic B	B-2
3.1.5	Understanding the Application frame	Basic	Unit 1, Topic B	B-1
3.2	**Importing and exporting presets**			
3.2.1	Knowing the location of preset files on both a PC and Mac platform	Basic	Unit 1, Topic C	
3.2.2	Understanding the process of exporting and importing presets	Basic	Unit 1, Topic C	C-2
3.3	**Resetting sliders and options**			
3.3.1	Working with sliders and buttons	Basic	Unit 1, Topic C	C-1
3.3.2	Using Alt key combinations	Basic	Unit 1, Topic C	
3.3.3	Resetting parameters	Basic	Unit 1, Topic C	C-2
3.3.4	Using Shift modifiers	Basic	Unit 1, Topic C	C-1
3.4	**Using tool groups and options**			
3.4.1	Selecting tools from a tool group	Basic	Unit 2, Topic A	A-1
3.4.2	Modifying individual tool options	Basic	Unit 1, Topic C	C-1
3.4.3	Creating tool presets	Basic	Unit 1, Topic C	C-1

4.0 Understanding selections

#	Objective	Course level	Conceptual information	Supporting activities
4.1	**Creating selections using appropriate tools**			
4.1.1	Creating selections with various tools and determining which selection tools work best for a given situation	Basic	Unit 2, Topic A	A-1, A-2
4.1.2	Working with the Quick Selection tool and options	Basic	Unit 2, Topic A	A-3
4.2	**Adding and subtracting from selections**			
4.2.1	Adding and subtracting selections	Basic	Unit 2, Topic B	B-1
4.2.2	Adding and subtracting of selections using different selection tools	Basic	Unit 2, Topic B	B-1
4.2.3	Modifying selections	Basic	Unit 2, Topic B	B-2
4.3	**Quick Mask usage**			
4.3.1	Creating a Quick Mask from a selection	Advanced	Unit 3, Topic A	A-1
4.3.2	Creating a blank Quick Mask	Advanced	Unit 3, Topic A	
4.3.3	Changing overlay	Advanced	Unit 3, Topic A	
4.3.4	Using brushes for addition to Quick Mask	Advanced	Unit 3, Topic A	A-1
4.3.5	Saving selections	Advanced	Unit 3, Topic A	A-2
4.4	**Using Refine Edge**			
4.4.1	Adjusting feather and smart radius	Advanced	Unit 3, Topic C	C-1
4.4.2	Masking to new layers or new channels	Advanced	Unit 3, Topic C	C-1
4.4.3	Determining which images will best be served by Refine Edge	Advanced	Unit 3, Topic C	C-1
4.4.4	Creating selections that will best benefit from Refine Edge	Advanced	Unit 3, Topic C	C-1

5.0 Understanding layers

#	Objective	Course level	Conceptual information	Supporting activities
5.1	**Creating and organizing layers**			
5.1.1	Creating different types of layers and dragging under/over for visibility	Basic	Unit 3, Topic A	A-1, A-2, A-3
5.1.2	Hiding and showing layers	Basic	Unit 3, Topic A	A-1
5.1.3	Using keyboard shortcuts for moving and creating layers	Basic	Unit 3, Topic A	A-1, A-3
5.1.4	Dragging and dropping images between documents	Basic	Unit 3, Topic A	A-2
5.2	**Understanding the differences between raster and shape layers**			
5.2.1	Understanding vector layers in Photoshop	Advanced	Unit 4, Topic A	A-2
5.2.2	Understanding the benefits of vector layers	Advanced	Unit 4, Topic A	A-1, A-2
5.2.3	Comparing and contrasting raster vs. vector	Advanced	Unit 4, Topic A	A-1
5.3	**Understanding layer masks**			
5.3.1	Creating layer masks using Panels and shortcuts	Advanced	Unit 3, Topic B	B-1
5.3.2	Modifying layer masks using brush-based tools	Advanced	Unit 3, Topic B	B-2, B-4
5.3.3	Copying and moving layer masks	Advanced	Unit 3, Topic B	B-2
5.3.4	Understanding the relationship between layer masks and Quick Mask	Advanced	Unit 3, Topic B	
5.3.5	Using layer masks with vector images and type	Advanced	Unit 3, Topic B	B-3
5.4	**Searching for layers**			
5.4.1	Organizing documents that have many layers	Advanced	Unit 1, Topic A	
5.4.2	Using the layer search feature	Advanced	Unit 1, Topic A	A-3
5.5	**Understanding layer groups**			
5.5.1	Grouping Layers	Advanced	Unit 1, Topic A	A-1
5.5.2	Clipping Layers	Advanced	Unit 1, Topic A	A-2
5.5.3	Blend mode and masks using layer groups	Advanced	Unit 1, Topic A	
5.5.4	Considerations for designs when using layer groups	Advanced	Unit 1, Topic A	
5.5.5	Keyboard shortcuts for grouping layers	Advanced	Unit 1, Topic A	A-1
5.6	**Understanding layer blend modes**			
5.6.1	Toggling blend modes using keyboard shortcuts	Advanced	Unit 1, Topic B	B-1
5.6.2	Explanation of blend mode functions and usage	Advanced	Unit 1, Topic B	B-1
5.6.3	Blend modes as they apply to video and design	Production	Unit 6, Topic A	

6.0 Understanding adjustments

#	Objective	Course level	Conceptual information	Supporting activities
6.1	**Differentiating between adjustment types**			
6.1.1	Identifying the strengths and weaknesses of specific adjustments	Basic	Unit 4, Topic A	A-1, A-2, A-3
		Advanced	Unit 2, Topic C	C-3, C-4
6.1.2	Applying adjustment layers for dramatic effect or color correction	Basic	Unit 4, Topic A Unit 4, Topic B	A-1 B-1
		Advanced	Unit 2, Topic C	C-3, C-4
6.1.3	Blending adjustment types	Advanced	Unit 2, Topic C	C-3
6.2	**Using TAT, clipping, and visibility**			
6.2.1	Working with the TAT	Basic	Unit 4, Topic B	B-2
6.3	**Refining masks on adjustments**			
6.3.1	Refining masks using the Density, Mask Edge, and Refine Mask options found in the Mask Properties panel	Advanced	Unit 3, Topic B	B-2

7.0 Editing images

#	Objective	Course level	Conceptual information	Supporting activities
7.1	**Working with the retouching tools**			
7.1.1	Using Dodge, Burn, Smudge, Blur	Basic	Unit 5, Topic B	B-1, B-2
7.1.2	Edge smoothing techniques	Basic	Unit 5, Topic B	B-2
7.1.3	Using the Clone Stamp, History Brush, and Sponge	Basic	Unit 5, Topic B	B-4, B-5
7.2	**Working with Liquify**			
7.2.1	Using the Liquify tool for correcting a photographic image or for special effect	Advanced	Unit 5, Topic B	B-1
7.2.2	Understanding the Liquify tool with regards to brush size and GPU acceleration	Advanced	Unit 5, Topic B	
7.2.3	Understanding Freeze/Thaw	Advanced	Unit 5, Topic B	B-1
7.3	**Using the transform controls**			
7.3.1	Using the transform controls to scale, rotate, and copy images	Basic	Unit 3, Topic B	B-1, B-2
7.3.2	Using keyboard modifier combinations for effective usage	Basic	Unit 3, Topic B	B-1
7.4	**Using Puppet Warp**			
7.4.1	Using the Puppet Warp tool to correct image problems in people and landscape-based images	Advanced	Unit 5, Topic A	A-3
7.4.2	Understanding how to add/removal points	Advanced	Unit 5, Topic A	A-3
7.4.3	Understanding the increase/decrease of mesh for maximum effective use	Advanced	Unit 5, Topic A	A-3

#	Objective	Course level	Conceptual information	Supporting activities
7.5	**Using the Clone Source panel**			
7.5.1	Understanding how to the use the clone source tool	Basic	Unit 5, Topic B	B-4
7.5.2	Understanding horizontal vertical offsets	Basic	Unit 5, Topic B	
7.5.3	Understanding rotation	Basic	Unit 5, Topic B	
7.5.4	Cloning images from separate documents	Basic	Unit 5, Topic B	
7.6	**Creating panoramas**			
7.6.1	Creating panoramas effectively by understanding Perspective, Cylindrical, Reposition, and other layers	Production	Unit 2, Topic A	A-1
7.6.2	Understanding geometric distortion correction and layer blending	Production	Unit 2, Topic A	A-1
7.6.3	Understanding the Adaptive Wide angle tool and its use in extreme panoramic and wide angle lens scenarios	Production	Unit 2, Topic A	A-2
7.7	**Using HDR Pro**			
7.7.1	Best practices for HDR generation	Production	Unit 2, Topic B	B-1
7.7.2	32-bit HDR creation	Production	Unit 2, Topic B	B-1
7.7.3	Tone control usage	Production	Unit 2, Topic B	B-1, B-2
7.7.4	Developing presets	Production	Unit 2, Topic B	B-2
7.7.5	Using ghosting source image alignment and post processing of the image	Production	Unit 2, Topic B	B-1, B-2
7.8	**Creating specialty images (black and white and duotone)**			
7.8.1	Best practices for creating black and white and duotone specialty images in Photoshop using Adjustment Layers and the Image > Mode command settings	Advanced	Unit 5, Topic C	C-1, C-3, C-4
7.8.2	Using a Black & White Adjustment layer	Advanced	Unit 5, Topic C	C-1
7.8.3	Using the Targeted Adjustment Tool	Advanced	Unit 5, Topic C	C-1
7.8.4	Using layer blending	Advanced	Unit 5, Topic C	
7.8.5	Using the Channel Mixer	Advanced	Unit 5, Topic C	
7.9	**Selecting color**			
7.9.1	Best practices for selecting color in an image and working with the appropriate color adjustment tools to isolate color casts for removal	Advanced	Unit 2, Topic C	C-1, C-2, C-3
7.9.2	Creating single color images and spot color designs	Advanced	Unit 2, Topic C	C-4, C-5
7.9.3	Adjusting colors that are out of gamut	Basic	Unit 5, Topic D	D-1

8.0 Working with design and print production

#	Objective	Course level	Conceptual information	Supporting activities
8.1	**Using character and paragraph styles**			
8.1.1	Creating and modifying character and paragraph styles	Basic	Unit 3, Topic C	C-3
8.1.2	Best practices for creating reusable styles	Basic	Unit 3, Topic C	
8.1.3	Clearing style formats from a documents	Basic	Unit 3, Topic C	
8.1.4	Font usage considerations	Basic	Unit 3, Topic C	
8.1.5	OpenType considerations	Basic	Unit 3, Topic C	
8.2	**Using vector shapes**			
8.2.1	Creating and modifying vector shapes	Advanced	Unit 4, Topic B	B-4
8.2.2	Modifying stroke and fill	Advanced	Unit 4, Topic B	B-5
8.2.3	Creating pen-based shapes	Advanced	Unit 4, Topic B	B-1, B-3
8.2.4	Stroking a path	Advanced	Unit 4, Topic B	B-5
8.2.5	Appending and inserting custom shapes	Advanced	Unit 4, Topic B	B-4
8.3	**Working with layer comps**			
8.3.1	Creating layer comps	Advanced	Unit 1, Topic D	D-1
8.3.2	Specifying what changes in a layer comp	Advanced	Unit 1, Topic D	D-1
8.3.3	Updating changes in layer comps	Advanced	Unit 1, Topic D	D-1
8.4	**Creating frame based animations**			
8.4.1	Specifying looping	Production	Unit 5, Topic C	C-1, C-4
8.4.2	Exporting frame based animations	Production	Unit 5, Topic C	C-4
8.5	**Working with layer styles**			
8.5.1	Accessing layer styles from multiple areas in Photoshop	Basic	Unit 3, Topic D	D-2
8.5.2	Adding several styles threaded together to create a specific style	Basic	Unit 3, Topic D	D-2

9.0 Working with video

#	Objective	Course level	Conceptual information	Supporting activities
9.1	**Ingesting video into Photoshop**			
9.1.1	Specifying supported video types	Production	Unit 6, Topic A	A-1
9.1.2	Tagging and metadata inspection of media images	Production	Unit 6, Topic A	
9.1.3	Creating video layers	Production	Unit 6, Topic A	A-2
9.2	**Cutting and trimming video**			
9.2.1	Using the Trim and Scrub feature	Production	Unit 6, Topic B	B-1, B-2
9.2.2	Specifying optimal sizes for playback, audio usage and fade/mute of audio	Production	Unit 6, Topic B	B-4
9.3	**Creating transitions within clips**			
9.3.1	Creating transitions between movie clips and other assets in a Photoshop video file	Production	Unit 6, Topic C	C-1
9.3.2	Explain cross transition to design elements, blending, layer stack usage, trimming, and effect transitions	Production	Unit 6, Topic C	C-1
9.4	**Adding design elements into video**			
9.4.1	Adding graphics	Production	Unit 6, Topic D	D-1
9.4.2	Adding text layers for titling	Production	Unit 6, Topic D	D-2
9.4.3	Working with 3D elements and textures for use in video	Production	Unit 6, Topic D	
9.4.4	Understanding the differences between video timelines and regular layers	Production	Unit 6, Topic D	
9.4.5	Considerations when using ripple delete	Production	Unit 6, Topic D	
9.4.6	Keyframing events	Production	Unit 6, Topic D	D-4
9.5	**Exporting and publishing video**			
9.5.1	Using Adobe Media Encoder	Production	Unit 6, Topic D	E-2
9.5.2	Specifying a preset	Production	Unit 6, Topic D	E-2
9.5.3	Using a built in preset for upload to commercial site	Production	Unit 6, Topic D	E-2
9.5.4	Using Photoshop Image Sequence	Production	Unit 6, Topic D	
9.5.5	Using the DPX Format	Production	Unit 6, Topic D	
9.6	**Using LUT adjustments for style**			
9.6.1	Defining Color Look Up Tables (LUT)	Production	Unit 6, Topic E	E-1
9.6.2	Explain how the LUT applies to images and video in Photoshop	Production	Unit 6, Topic E	
9.6.3	Explain how to import LUT files for use in Photoshop	Production	Unit 6, Topic E	

10.0 Outputting for Web, print, and mobile

#	Objective	Course level	Conceptual information	Supporting activities
10.1	**Differentiating between file types**			
10.1.1	Understanding the differences between TIF, JPG, PNG, GIF, PSD, PSB, and other file types	Basic	Unit 1, Topic A	A-1. A-2
10.1.2	Understanding which file type to choose for a given scenario	Basic	Unit 1, Topic A	A-1, A-2
10.2	**Using Save For Web**			
10.2.1	Using Save For Web for clearing metadata	Production	Unit 5, Topic A	A-1, A-4
10.2.2	Applying color profiles	Production	Unit 5, Topic A	A-4
10.2.3	Specifying file sizes	Production	Unit 5, Topic A	A-2, A-6
10.2.4	2 up 4 up comparisons	Production	Unit 5, Topic A	A-4
10.2.5	Considerations regarding speed and download for images on the Web	Production	Unit 5, Topic A	A-1, A-3
10.3	**Using the Print dialog**			
10.3.1	Setting up appropriate color spaces for proofing	Production	Unit 3, Topic C	C-2
10.3.2	Using ICC profiles	Production	Unit 3, Topic C	C-1, C-2, C-3
10.3.3	Creating custom paper types	Production	Unit 3, Topic C	C-1, C-2
10.3.4	Selecting the appropriate rendering intent	Production	Unit 3, Topic C	C-2
10.3.5	Checking for out of gamut colors	Production	Unit 3, Topic C	C-2
10.3.6	Simulating black ink	Production	Unit 3, Topic C	C-1

Course summary

This summary contains information to help you bring the course to a successful conclusion. Using this information, you will be able to:

A Use the summary text to reinforce what you've learned in class.

B Determine the next courses in this series (if any), as well as any other resources that might help you continue to learn about Adobe Photoshop CS6.

Topic A: Course summary

Use the following summary text to reinforce what you've learned in class.

Unit summaries

Unit 1

In this unit, you learned about using different **file types** in Photoshop. Then you learned how to switch **screen modes**, arrange **panels**, and save a panel arrangement as a **workspace**. You also **magnified** an image and **scrolled** to view different parts of it. You also learned how to set up **rulers**, **guides**, and **grids**. Finally, you learned how to specify **tool options**, and you created and exported a **tool preset**.

Unit 2

In this unit, you used the **marquee** tools, the **Lasso** tool, and the **Quick Selection** tool to select image areas. You also **added to and subtracted from a selection** and modified a selection by applying **feathering**

Unit 3

In this unit, you created and transformed **layers**, changed the layer **stacking order**, and created **type layers**. In addition, you adjusted layer **opacity**, and you used the Layer Style dialog box to apply **layer styles**, such as outlines, glows, and shadows.

Unit 4

In this unit, you specified an automatic adjustment to an **adjustment layer**. You also used the **target point tools** to specify an image's target highlights and shadows. Next, you used a **Curves adjustment layer** to adjust image contrast and used the **Targeted Adjustment tool**. You also applied a **clipping mask** to an adjustment layer.

Unit 5

In this unit, you repaired **image defects** by using the Red Eye, Spot Healing Brush, and Patch tools. You also **retouched images** by using the Burn, Blur, Content-Aware Move, Clone Stamp, and History Brush tools. In addition, you used the **Background Eraser tool**, and you learned how to use **Content-Aware Fill**. You also selected colors and **painted** in an image. Finally, you applied **filters** to layers.

Unit 6

In this unit, you determined an image's **dimensions** and **resolution**. You also resized images, with and without **resampling**. Finally, you used the Crop tool and the Canvas Size dialog box to change an image's **canvas size**.

Unit 7

In this unit, you learned how to **import images** from a digital camera into Bridge and how to use Bridge to **navigate your computer's folder structure**. Then you used **Review Mode** to preview files. You also viewed and added **metadata** and created **keywords** and added them to images. Then you used metadata to **find** and **filter** files in Bridge. Next, you organized files in Bridge by creating **collections**. Finally, you output files by creating a **PDF contact sheet** and a **Web gallery**.

Topic B: Continued learning after class

It is impossible to learn how to use any software effectively in a single day. To get the most out of this class, you should begin working with Photoshop CS6 to perform real tasks as soon as possible. We also offer resources for continued learning.

Next courses in this series

This is the first course in this series. The next courses in this series are:

- *Photoshop CS6: Advanced, ACE Edition*
- *Photoshop CS6: Production, ACE Edition*

Other resources

For more information on this and other topics, go to **www.Crisp360.com**.

Crisp360 is an online community where you can expand your knowledge base, connect with other professionals, and purchase individual training solutions.

Glossary

Adjustment layer

A layer that applies color and contrast changes to underlying layers without changing the actual pixels on those layers (i.e., nondestructively).

Anti-aliasing

The softening of selected edges by applying varying levels of transparency to pixels along the edge of the selection.

Application frame

The window containing all the elements of the Photoshop interface. On Mac computers, it can be turned on or off.

Canvas

The full editable area of an image.

Character style

A set of text formatting that you can save and apply to individually selected characters as desired.

Contrast

The difference in brightness between the dark and light areas in an image.

Crop

To enlarge or reduce the size of an image's canvas. Typically, cropping removes some image pixels while retaining the rest without resampling, but you can also rotate and change the resolution of an image as you crop it.

Destructive edits

Edits to an image that result in a permanent change to the image's pixels.

Feathering

A setting that blends a selection with its background by applying transparency to the selection's outer pixels.

Filter

An effect that changes pixel colors permanently. Filters range from artistic effects that can dramatically change an image's appearance, to subtle ones used to affect characteristics like sharpness and contrast.

Floating selection

A selection that you move in an image.

Gamma

A control that affects the midtone brightness in an image. Gamma values above 1.0 brighten the midtones, and values below 1.0 darken them.

Gamut

The total range of colors that a device or image can display.

GIF format

A format with a single 8-bit channel that can hold up to 256 colors, including transparency. GIF images are best used for illustrations that have few colors and that are intended for display on the Web.

Highlight

Either a very light image area, or the very lightest pixel in an image.

Histogram

A graph representing the number of pixels at each brightness level in an image. Photoshop displays histograms in the Levels dialog box, the Histogram panel, and in the Properties panel when a Levels adjustment layer is selected.

Image resolution

The number of pixels per inch (ppi) at which the image will be printed. Alternately, the pixel dimensions (such as 1600×1200 pixels) in an image, regardless of the ppi value.

JPEG format

An image format that applies lossy compression to reduce file size at the expense of image quality. Low-resolution, low-quality JPEG images are best used for Web display, while high-resolution, high-quality JPEG images can be suitable for printing.

Lossless compression

A method of reducing an image's file size that does not change the original pixels or reduce image quality.

Lossy compression

A method of reducing an image's file size by altering pixel colors in a way that reduces image quality.

Metadata

Information stored along with an image, typically with descriptive keywords and data about the image's source, purpose, or digital camera settings.

Midtones

Image areas that are neither very dark nor very bright.

Mini Bridge

Panel appearing at the bottom of the default Essentials workspace with which you can access Adobe Bridge features.

Nondestructive effect

An effect, such as a blending mode, that doesn't permanently alter the pixels in the image.

Opacity

The degree of "solidity" of a pixel or layer. Items with 100% opacity are completely opaque, while lower-opacity items are semi-transparent.

Paragraph style

A set of text formatting that you can save and apply to paragraphs as desired.

Paragraph text

Text that can wrap in multiple lines within a rectangular shape in Photoshop.

Pixelation

The jagged, stair-step appearance that occurs when you can see an image's individual pixels. With a high enough image resolution, you can avoid pixelation.

PNG format

Image format that supports more than 16 million colors, uses a variety of lossless compression algorithms, and supports many levels of transparency. Suitable for Web and for print use, although some Web browsers might not support its transparency settings.

Point text

Text that appears within a single line in Photoshop.

Printer resolution

The number of ink dots per inch (dpi) that a device can print. Printer resolution differs from image resolution, which is measured in pixels per inch (ppi).

PSD format

Native file format in Photoshop that preserves layers, effects, adjustments, etc.

Resampling

The process of adding or removing image pixels while trying to retain the original image's appearance. Photoshop resamples images when you change the resolution or image dimensions independently from one another.

Rule of thirds

A design principle (employed by default when using the Crop tool) whereby an image is divided into imaginary gridlines separating the image into thirds horizontally and vertically. Important compositional elements could be placed at the intersections of the lines or within the boxes formed by the grid.

Sampling

Copying the pixels from one area of an image so that they can be applied to another area, as with the Clone Stamp tool.

Scrubbing

Dragging a setting's label to change the value in Photoshop. For example, you can drag the word "Opacity" rather using the slider or entering a value.

Shadow

Either a very dark image area, or the very darkest pixel in an image.

Specular highlight

Reflected light from a shiny surface. You can usually allow specular highlights to appear pure white.

TIFF format

A file format typically used for printed images. A TIFF file can support lossless and lossy compression and can hold either a flattened or layered image.

Workspace

A particular arrangement of panels, keyboard shortcuts, and menus in Photoshop that can be saved and reused.

Index